A Sampling of Endorsements from Pastors, Ministry Leaders, and Clinicians Across Many Streams of the Church

In a world that often makes a hard distinction between the empirical data of psychology and the theology of the church, this book says that these two worlds can coexist and be used for the glory of God. I am grateful to call Shaunti and Jim and The Church Cares partners in ministry as we journey with people in their pain and make much of the name of Jesus.

MATT CARTER
Therapist and director of pastoral care at Passion City Church, Atlanta, Georgia

This book is a road map with invaluable insights on positioning and equipping the church for best practices in mental health ministry and building a CARE ministry. This framework will make a profound difference and ultimately transform how the church addresses mental health.

REINA OLMEDA
Director of the Mental Health Initiative for the National Hispanic Christian Leadership Conference; author of *Fit for Your Assignment*; professional counselor

This book includes practical tools, biblical wisdom, and a clear framework for building a mental health ministry. I fully endorse this book as a must-read for anyone committed to the emotional and spiritual well-being of their community, whether you are just beginning or looking to strengthen an existing ministry.

STEVEN BALDWIN
Pastoral care pastor, Apostolic Faith Church, Chicago, Illinois

Training laypeople to care for the hurting is a vision right out of Jesus' playbook. Feldhahn and Sells root their plan in solid research and timeless wisdom. Our fifty-plus years of experience in both evangelical and Catholic churches confirm that this kind of care is desperately needed in our current mental health crisis.

ERICK AND ELIZABETH SCHENKEL
Vice president of Biblical Engagement, Global2033 (Catholic consortium); former executive director (Erick) and current content leader (Elizabeth), *Jesus* Film Project

When Hurting People Come to Church by Shaunti Feldhahn and James Sells is an excellent, clearly written, biblically based, comprehensive, and helpful book with many practical guidelines. It is a must-read for all churches and Christians wanting to be effective helpers and contributors in dealing with the current mental health crisis. Highly recommended!

REVEREND SIANG-YANG TAN, PhD
Senior professor of clinical psychology, Fuller Theological Seminary; author of *Lay Counseling* (with Eric Scalise) and *Counseling and Psychotherapy: A Christian Perspective*

A vast number of people today are experiencing extreme distress and disturbance in their souls. Feldhahn and Sells use research and biblical scholarship to highlight the problem and propose solutions. The central thesis: *The church* should be leading the charge in providing care for hurting people. The current mental health crisis should not scare Christians but inspire us to action.

CURTIS W. SOLOMON, MDiv, ThM, PhD
Executive director of the Biblical Counseling Coalition; author of *I Have PTSD: Reorienting After Trauma*

In a time when mental health needs are frequently described as at a crisis state, Feldhahn and Sells offer a passionate, hopeful, and practical primer on how churches can be a major resource for meeting these needs. Community psychology has long championed the importance of cultivating natural helping networks to meet the large-scale psychological needs of our world. This text presents a compelling vision for how one of the world's largest such networks may achieve just that.

WILLIAM L. HATHAWAY, PhD
Provost, Regent University

Feldhahn and Sells have published the most practical mental health/care ministry aid for pastors that I have come across. As a denominational leader, I can say that it will give a very sound structure to the pastoral care strategy of any church, regardless of size or denomination.

PAUL KUZMA, MA, BCPC, PSAP
Director, Center for Spiritual Renewal East, The Foursquare Church

As a mental health professional and practice director who works with both Catholic and Protestant churches, I appreciate the thorough research (they polled 2,000 pastors, church leaders, and clinicians!), the survey data (which highlights the needs of pastors and ministry leaders), and the case studies of churches that have successfully implemented a mental health ministry. This timely book also provides an overview of basic skills related to being present, being an active listener, learning emotional regulation, fostering relational growth, responding to trauma and grief, and helping those dealing with addictions. I believe any church will find value in this insightful and readable book.

GERRY KEN CRETE, PhD, LPC, LMFT
Founder of Transfiguration Counseling and Coaching; cofounder of Souls and Hearts; author of *Litanies of the Heart: Relieving Post-Traumatic Stress and Calming Anxiety Through Healing Our Parts*

When Hurting People Come to Church inspires pastors, ministry leaders, and church members alike to embrace their role in the crucial mental health journey of care. If the church is truly called to be the hands and feet of Christ, it cannot afford to ignore the mental and emotional struggles of its people and the community at large. This book is a must-read for anyone who desires to see the church become not just a place of worship but a sanctuary of healing, restoration, and hope.

REVEREND N. CHARLES OLMEDA, PhD
Lead co-pastor of Transformation Church, Allentown, Pennsylvania; board member of the National Hispanic Christian Leadership Conference

Pastors often feel overwhelmed and ill-equipped to deal with the increasing occurrences of mental health concerns among their church members. Theologically insightful, deeply rooted in the gospel, and written with great care and expertise, *When Hurting People Come to Church* is an essential book that every pastor and church worker who is seeking to care for their members should read.

CORNÉ J. BEKKER
Dean and professor, Regent University School of Divinity

WHEN HURTING PEOPLE COME TO CHURCH

SHAUNTI FELDHAHN & JAMES N. SELLS

When Hurting People Come to Church

How People of Faith Can Help Solve the **MENTAL HEALTH CRISIS**

Visit Tyndale online at tyndale.com.

Visit Shaunti Feldhahn online at shaunti.com.

Visit James N. Sells at thechurchcares.com.

Tyndale, Tyndale's quill logo, *Tyndale Refresh*, and the Tyndale Refresh logo are registered trademarks of Tyndale House Ministries. Tyndale Refresh is a nonfiction imprint of Tyndale House Publishers, Carol Stream, Illinois.

When Hurting People Come to Church: How People of Faith Can Help Solve the Mental Health Crisis

Cover design by Libby Dykstra

Interior design by Brandi Davis

Edited by Stephanie Rische

For information about special discounts for bulk purchases, please contact Tyndale House Publishers at csresponse@tyndale.com, or call 1-855-277-9400.

Library of Congress Cataloging-in-Publication Data

A catalog record for this book is available from the Library of Congress.

ISBN 979-8-4005-0948-3

Printed in the United States of America

31 30 29 28 27 26 25
7 6 5 4 3 2 1

To those who pour themselves out like a drink offering. The world will never truly know all that you give every day. But there is One who does.

Contents

Foreword

This landmark book addresses the panic almost every pastor I know faces, one I faced personally for decades: the overwhelming pastoral needs people have.

When it comes to tackling the challenges of human needs, I have noticed two broad approaches that pastors take.

One is what I learned to do: refer almost any need either to the group's ministry in our church or to a professional counselor outside our church. We'd even pay for the first few sessions, if need be. Not everyone is a fan of this approach, but given my personality, my lack of training in counseling, and the size of our church, it was the best I could do.

The second approach is more common among pastors of smaller churches who are wired as shepherds. Their response? Take on as many counseling appointments as they can, often to the point of exhaustion or burnout.

Neither model is ideal. In the first case, it's likely that a lot of pastoral care needs remain functionally unaddressed. In the second approach, not only does the pastor get overwhelmed, but it's unlikely that a single pastor or staff team can adequately address the multiplicity of issues people face.

If this weren't challenging enough, start adding AI into the mix. The twenty-first century is already the loneliest century in history, and technology that is designed to keep us connected is instead making us even more lonely, isolated, and depressed.

Fortunately, none of this surprises God. He designed the church for such a time as this. The model that Shaunti Feldhahn and James Sells propose is something that every church leader should study, embrace, and adopt.

You'll find numerous surprises in this book and repeatedly notice yourself nodding in agreement. Regardless of your church's size, style, resources, geography, or demographic, you'll find practical steps to help your people thrive again—mentally, emotionally, and spiritually.

One of my favorite aspects of this book is that I believe it will kick-start deeper discipleship and better evangelism in your church—two infusions most churches need.

Another favorite aspect? It's short. On behalf of every busy church leader, thank you, Shaunti and Jim, for not making this landmark work longer than it needs to be.

My only regret? I wish I had this book when I was leading our church.

Carey Nieuwhof
Author, podcaster, and speaker
Founding pastor, Connexus Church

PART 1

A New Model of Care

1

A New Way Through

How the Church Can Stand in the Gap for Mental Health

The boy clambered up the heights until he reached the hole.
His chubby little finger was thrust in, almost before he knew it.
The flowing was stopped!

"Ah!" he thought, with a chuckle of boyish delight, "the angry waters must stay back now! Haarlem shall not be drowned while *I* am here!"

MARY MAPES DODGE, *Hans Brinker: Or, The Silver Skates*

Pastor Brent has his finger in the dike, as if he is holding back the North Sea. He is the family pastor of a community-oriented church.[1] They preach and pray, marry and bury, and everything in between. He loves his work and he loves his community, but he is overwhelmed. For years now, ministry has been endless variations on a single theme: people need help.

- They need help in their marriages.
- Help in overcoming addictions to substances, behaviors, and lifestyles.
- Help in caring for children or aging parents.
- Help in managing money.

- Help in the anxiety of facing cancer.
- Help in facing depression after losing someone to cancer.
- Help in confronting loneliness, trauma, or fighting temptation.
- Help in recovering after failing to fight off temptation.
- Help in confronting the lie that they should be able to handle it by themselves.

These needs are, after all, among the reasons Brent became a pastor. He wants to help people's lives be transformed by the power of the gospel.

So, he is a student on how to help well and how to keep himself from burning out. He reads books about pastoral boundaries, has regular date nights with his wife, and meets with a group of guys to pray and talk about the challenges of ministry. These things are helpful. Yet the responsibility remains, and the calls asking for help keep coming at rates beyond his capacity.

Brent does what he can, and he meets with a steady stream of people to listen, pray, and plan. He refers many of them to trusted therapists when the need is beyond his schedule or skill. But these professionals are often full, or costly.

Often, there is nothing else he can do to help. Sometimes the church pays for the first therapy session. But what happens during the weeks or months while they wait? What happens when the person can't afford more than one or two sessions?

He feels like his people are often fending for themselves. The phrase "be warm and be filled" keeps him awake at night.

Brent knows ministry is God's calling for him, yet he frequently feels discouraged. He wonders if there's a different way to bring aid, comfort, and direction to those who follow Jesus—and those who need to know Him.

For Those on the Front Lines

This book is for those with their fingers in the dike. We are offering a practical, doable way through the challenges faced by pastors, priests, deacons, elders, church leaders, ministry leaders, and clinicians who work or volunteer in the church to care for the hurting but find the scope overwhelming.

While Pastor Brent may not realize it, he is on the front lines of a silent war that's being waged inside and outside the church today. Researchers call it a mental health crisis. Pastors, therapists, and ministry leaders call it exhausting.

Perhaps that's you.

Every day, you may resonate with Paul's words: "There is the daily pressure on me of my anxiety for all the churches" (2 Corinthians 11:28).

This book aims to help you alleviate that pressure and anxiety, ensuring that more people are helped—and helped better. In our broken world, the pressure of ministry will always be there to some degree, but it does not have to be to *this* degree.

About Us and Our Research

You might be wondering, *Who are these authors who are not pastors or church leaders and are proposing a different way for those who are?*

We are your fans. We are your greatest supporters. We work in the church and ministry space every day, and we see the burden you carry.

You are the boots on the ground, doing the work of the Kingdom, and we want to help. One of us (Jim) is a licensed psychologist and a leader at a Christian university who prepares mental health professionals to care for others and codirects a research center that creates resources for everything related to marriage, family, the church, and mental health. The other (Shaunti) is a longtime ministry leader and author of dozens of books. Both of us are also researchers who have investigated the current challenge facing the church and possible solutions by seeking input and hearing the perspectives of more than 2,000 leaders and professionals like you.

We conducted a national survey of nearly 1,900 pastors, priests, church leaders, and clinicians about mental health in the church,[2] and we personally interviewed and spoke with hundreds more. (For simplicity's sake, throughout the book, we refer to clergy across all streams of the church as pastors.)

In the process, we have seen and heard how leaders in many streams of the church view mental health and create care. Based on this data, we have also seen many examples of innovative ministry emerging, and a new way forward that will help you, the people you serve, and the church as a whole. This will not replace the ministry of care you are called to but will enrich it—and hopefully even expand it.

Our goal is to help you think through this new way forward and show how it might work for you in very practical ways. Just as you feel strongly called to help care for others, we feel called to help care for you. God cares about His leaders and caregivers in the church, and He sees all that you are carrying!

We should mention that the survey data, along with many helpful resources—including appendix 2 of this book, which offers a curated, practical list for churches—is available at Thechurchcares.com. You will read more about The Church Cares, the initiative and organization we help lead, in later chapters.[3]

What's Causing the Mental Health Crisis—and How Can the Church Be a Solution?

The 2023 warning from Thomas Insel, the former director of the National Institute of Mental Health, was pretty stark:

> Our nation is facing a new public health threat. . . . Feelings of anxiety and depression have grown to levels where virtually no one can ignore what is happening. . . . Ninety percent of Americans feel we are in a mental health crisis.[4]

They are right. The evidence from both clinical research and government assessment indicates a rapid increase in prevalence, need, and cost of mental health services in virtually every category (e.g., suicide, addiction, and trauma) and virtually every demographic and age group. There are many reasons for this crisis, both within the church and in society at large. Countless studies have looked at factors as diverse as marital breakdown, the prevalence of racial injustice, and the use of smartphones at key stages of emotional development.

It's likely that any number of factors may be contributing. But we propose that underneath all of that are two major cultural reasons for the pressure you feel—and one way the church can be a transformative solution for each of them.

Issue #1: So Many People in Need, So Few to Help

The movie *Gone with the Wind*, set during the Civil War, has come under scrutiny in recent years due to its damaging racial stereotypes. Midway through the movie, there is an illustration of a different type of damage. This scene shows wounded soldiers being cared for by desperate nurses, wives, mothers, all trying to respond to a cacophony of pleas for aid. As the camera draws further and further back, the wounded are revealed to be in the hundreds . . . then thousands . . . all calling for the help of a few caregivers. The viewer is confronted with the enormity of human carnage.

In the twenty-first century, so are we.

In this book, we write of a similar scene—just with a different type of wounded. When we refer to those with mental health concerns, we mean anyone in mental, emotional, and/or spiritual distress. This could be the man whose marriage is falling apart, the woman with an eating disorder, the bullied teenager with social anxiety, the retiree with depression, the military veteran with PTSD, the single mom who just lost her job, the long-married couple who hasn't had sex in five years, or the newlywed who is wrestling with critical in-laws. When you zoom out, you can see the enormity of human carnage. And they are all calling for the help of too few caregivers.

For fifty years, society has created a professionalized mental health culture as the primary means of caring for those in distress.[5] Initially, in order to access insurance coverage, the counseling profession began redefining most psychological needs as having a medical pathology. But over time, this resulted in licensed counseling becoming the standard of care for all life stressors.

Now, just to be clear: much about the rise of skilled professionals has been extremely helpful. Sophisticated, empirically validated research has uncovered key ways to address mental health disorders and challenging life issues. Specialists apply precision and clarity to complex problems. And state licensing standards ensure that therapists have a high level of training, skill, and ethical adherence.

To speak directly to the clinician: you have made a significant difference in the lives of untold numbers because of your expertise and care.

The downside of this trend, however, is that vast numbers of people—those with diagnosable disorders and those with significant life pain—flood therapists' offices. With therapy as the treatment path for all levels of pain, the capacity for care is overwhelmed. Imagine the panic of a parent whose eighth grader deeply struggles with academic anxiety and needs a counselor but must wait three months for an appointment. Three months! By that time, the child may have failed the eighth grade and internalized the idea that nothing is ever going to change.

It's a classic supply and demand problem. It's a lot like what happened on my (Jim's) hometown's Southern California roads: freeways have been expanded to twenty-six lanes but are *still* inadequate to accommodate the cars that flood the region. The problem isn't just that there aren't enough lanes; it's that there are too many cars.

This is similar to what the church is facing. As we'll discuss more in chapter 3, there aren't nearly enough professionals to meet the demand in today's mental health culture—and there is an overwhelming need!

Here's one example, which I (Jim) shared in my 2024 book for clinicians, *Beyond the Clinical Hour*: among the forty million American adults with clinically significant anxiety, just fifteen million are getting help.[6] Fully twenty-five million—more than the population of Florida—are not. In many cases, this is because they can't find a mental health professional with capacity to see them or because they can't afford their services.

At the same time, a parallel trend has long been underway in the church. Because of the movement toward professionalism, we have become increasingly uncomfortable with addressing mental health concerns in churches. Like their secular counterparts in medicine, business, and education, most church leaders see "referring out" as the thing to do.

We often hear the rhyme that one pastor used on our survey, "When in doubt, refer out."

Thus, when help seekers come to the church, they may talk to a pastor, but much of the time they are also referred to a mental health professional. On our national survey, 67 percent of pastors and church leaders fully agreed with this statement: "If a person's presenting issue is primarily psychological rather than spiritual, the church's primary mental health service should be to refer to a mental health professional."[7] Only 12 percent disagreed with that statement.

"If a person's presenting issue is primarily psychological rather than spiritual, the church's primary mental health service should be to refer to a mental health professional."

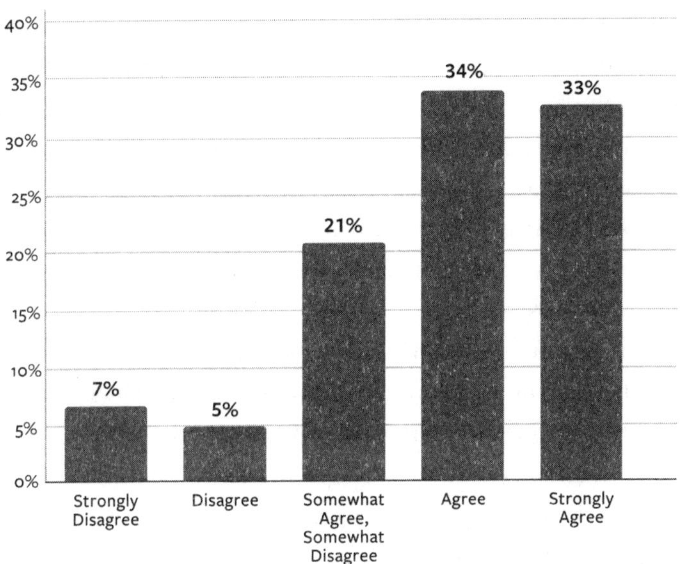

It's our perspective that referrals are indeed often needed. Yet there's an unintended consequence to this overall pattern of referring out: people are being funneled out and away from the church at a time when people need the church most! Of course, there are times when people need more help than a pastor or a ministry can provide, and throughout the book we offer guidance about when referrals are best. (You can see an overview of how to do referrals well and a referral decision tree in appendix 3 online at Thechurchcares.com.) But in many cases, churches are letting professionals do what the church was intended to do. Churches can reclaim their role by doing "referrals with" rather than "referrals out."

One pastor we spoke with said this realization was the catalyst for his church's creation of a mental health ministry. He explained, "Our reasoning was what you see when Jesus leaves the ninety-nine sheep to go after the one. This lost sheep needed more attention and care. So Jesus went after that sheep, carried it back, and now that sheep is *with* the flock. It's with the others as it receives care. Soon, the sheep is walking again. But when that sheep is broken, that's the time it needs to be carried the most."

Another consequence to referring out is the mental health equivalent of twenty-six packed lanes of traffic. There simply aren't enough professional providers to keep up with the current default of referring out. It's estimated that to reach the millions in need of care, hundreds of thousands of therapists[8] need to be trained at a cost of billions of dollars. The need is there, but the professional workforce and the money are not.

This might sound dire, but thankfully there is a solution to these dilemmas. To see it, let's start by looking through the eyes of Pastor Brent and others like him.

Pastor Brent's Tuesday Afternoon

Pastor Brent took the call and heard a very stressed female voice.

"Uh, hi. My name is Roni. My neighbor goes to your church and gave me your number. I am at the end." Roni began to cry as she told her story. "I'm caring for my two elderly parents with dementia. My husband is a cross-country truck driver, and he's only home about one week a month, so he can't really help. Last week my seventeen-year-old daughter told me she was pregnant. I haven't been able to sleep all week. We are a mess. I know I should see somebody, but I haven't a clue who to see, or how to afford it . . ."

Pastor Brent looked at his watch. It was 5:20 p.m. He sent up a silent prayer for wisdom and texted his wife a frequent code: "RN 60." That meant that something had come up RN—right now—and he would call in sixty minutes. They were used to it. It happened a lot.

Pastor Brent and Roni spoke for about forty-five minutes. He empathized with the heavy burdens she was carrying and reassured her that each could be addressed in the proper time. He confirmed that no one was going to hurt themselves and everyone was safe. He gave her two numbers to call: the crisis pregnancy hotline and a Christian counselor. He prayed with Roni and invited her to come to the office. It would have to be late the next week or maybe the week after, as there were other similar needs already crowding his schedule. He said goodbye, wishing he could do more. He knew he couldn't, but he also knew he was leaving Roni consumed with grief, confusion, despair, and loneliness.

He sent a text to the counselor telling her that Roni might be calling and asking if there was any way she could work her in, and then he hustled to the car, calling his wife to apologize and let her know he was on the way. As he drove on a hill overlooking thousands of houses in his valley, he was struck that somewhere in that view was Roni's house—and hundreds of other houses where pain, grief, and despair were served along with dinner. In exhaustion, he thought, *I have the power of the gospel to change hearts, restore the broken, and heal family wounds, yet I feel powerless.* As he pulled into his driveway, he thought, *I don't have time to do more. But is there a way I can do it differently?*

Before We Can Fix It, We Need to Understand It

This question about how the church can do things differently is the central theme of this book. To forge a new path with the current circumstances and resources, we must understand the problem underneath the problem in the church, in the mental health field, and in the culture at large. Both the problem and the solution can be captured by comparing two large triangles.

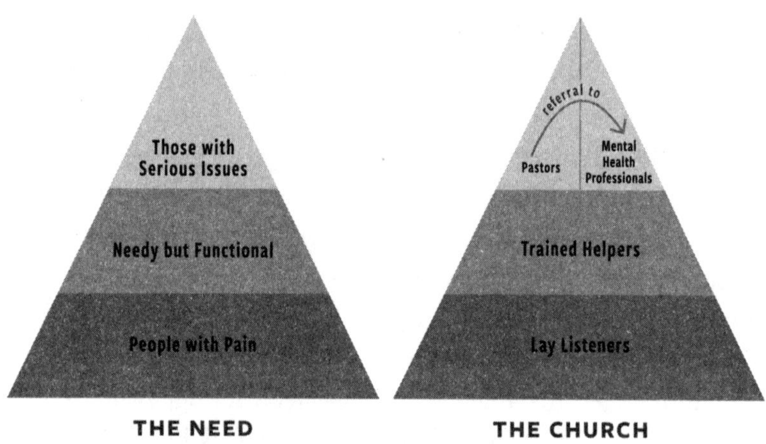

The first triangle represents the need within the church; it's what Pastor Brent experiences every week. At the top of the triangle are those with serious issues. These include marriages in extreme crisis, people whose addictions are blowing up their lives, those contemplating self-harm, those with psychiatric diseases that the industry labels as serious mental illnesses (SMI), such as bipolar disorder or debilitating major depression that prevents them from getting out of bed.[9] This group may not constitute a huge number within the congregation—perhaps 5 to 10 percent of the church—but they likely have significant, demanding, and often complex needs.

The second group in the need triangle, the needy but functional, is larger: about a fourth of the church and community. This group has serious needs or pain that requires ongoing attention, but they are generally able to live their lives. They may be depressed, but they go to work every day. They may be dealing with trauma, grief, divorce, bankruptcy, the loss of a child, or an addiction, and carrying these loads like rocks in a day pack, yet they can carry on. They may be on medication, or not. They may see a clinician, or not. From the outside you may or may not know the burden is there.

Then there's the big group at the bottom of the need triangle. These are people with pain—which includes all of us at various times. No one escapes it, whether we're facing marriage issues, singleness issues, parenting heartbreak, caregiving strain, grief, anxiety, illness, job loss, or finances. And when those challenges arise, we all need a place to go, a person to talk to, and a shoulder to cry on.

Thankfully, we don't need to be left alone with this weight.

While the need triangle describes three groups with varying levels of need, the second triangle is a depiction of the church and the helpers within it (or external helpers the church outsources to). It represents the help that is available to the hurting.

At the top of the triangle are pastors and mental health professionals. In the middle are what we might call trained helpers. These are the facilitators and the groups with some mental health training or experience, many of whom are specialized in a particular area of need. These might include mental health coaches, lay counselors, or leaders of groups like Alcoholics Anonymous, Celebrate Recovery, GriefShare, DivorceCare, or Pure Desire. More broadly, these might also include those who have been trained in life care and mentoring, such as Stephen Ministries leaders.

At the bottom of the church triangle is . . . everyone else. These are individuals who care about those around them and want to help. If you've been going through a hard time since your mother died and you need a friend to share an iced latte with on a Saturday afternoon, this is who you turn to. These are small group leaders, prayer warriors, caring grandparents, Sunday school teachers, Bible study members. This is the body of Christ.

A Picture of the Problem

In any given church, a small triangle of clinicians and pastors are trying to care for most of the population of people in need—handling big stuff and little stuff and everything in between. They are at the top of the mental health culture, and they're seen as the "fixers." So the default is to channel nearly every problem to them and through them.

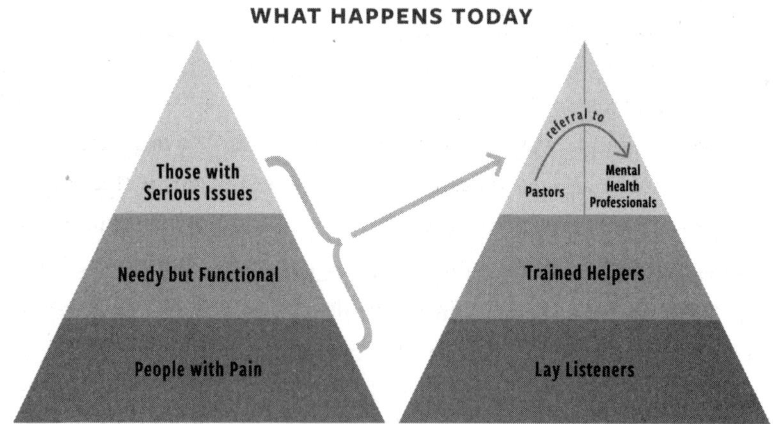

This is why Pastor Brent and mental health providers are overwhelmed. This explains the ache he experiences when people like Roni call. Most pastors resonate with the feeling of having few hours and fewer options to offer those who come to them for care: they typically talk to the person a few times and hope they can be seen by others for more extensive follow-up. They may also hope they can find some sort of group or social support for the person, but that is often hit or miss.

Now, we need to explicitly say that people turning to pastors and mental health providers is a *good* thing! Research indicates that most people improve in managing life crises at any level when they seek pastoral and/or clinical help. This is why I (Jim) have devoted more than thirty-five years to my calling as a counselor and counselor educator. Most pastors do a magnificent job in their role of pastoral counseling, which will always be needed. But the *default* of running everything through the top of the triangle has created the "fingers in the dike" problem. A lot of people need help, and there simply aren't enough people available to help.

A Picture of the Solution

There is a simple way of looking at the solution. We must enlist the entire church and *all* types of helpers. As indicated in this image, those with higher levels of specialization and training help those with more intense or more complex needs, and those with lower levels of specialization and training help those with lower-intensity needs.

We call this the church CARE strategy (Coordinated Attention, Restoration, and Encouragement). As you'll see in a moment, *this* is a solution for Pastor Brent when someone like Roni calls. It's the different way of doing things he's been seeking.

WHAT NEEDS TO HAPPEN

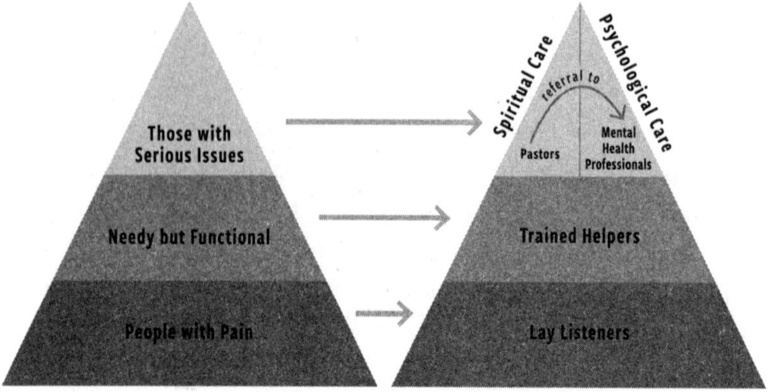

Those with Serious Issues
Needy but Functional
People with Pain

Spiritual Care
Psychological Care
referral to
Pastors
Mental Health Professionals
Trained Helpers
Lay Listeners

Let's return to Pastor Brent. Imagine that when he picks up the phone at 5:20 p.m. on Tuesday, he has already implemented the CARE strategy in his church. As he listens to Roni, he pictures the triangle and thinks through different types and levels of help. A clinician might be needed, but someone is also needed now to walk alongside her in her panic, grief, and worry. Although he cannot do that, there are others in his congregation who can.

After listening with compassion, offering wisdom, and praying for her, he tells her, "It will probably take me a week or two to see you, but in the meantime, I'm going to have our CARE coordinator call you tonight or tomorrow. She is a retired nurse who volunteers a few hours a week, and she will hear more about your story and make a plan with you for moving forward."

Pastor Brent knows that the CARE coordinator will assess the level of need and care available, and then refer Roni to a trained lay listener who can come alongside her. She might connect Roni with a small group or a community resource. And she will determine whether Roni needs to see a mental health professional.

A Simple Change with a Big Impact

Adding these levels of care—the coordinator role, trained helpers, and lay listeners—allows churches to always be present for others. This CARE strategy creates opportunities for ongoing support rather than funneling people like Roni away from the church.

Many churches (62 percent, on our survey) already offer some kind of trained helper care, often through specialized groups such as recovery programs. But comparatively few (25 percent) have any type of organization around lay listening. The lay listener level of care is the most needed—and it's the easiest to recruit and support participants for. And with training in some basic skills (which will be covered in later chapters, such as knowing when to refer), it can also be safe and incredibly effective for leveraging the resources already available. One of the best informal counselors I (Jim) have ever known was my grandmother, who used just an eighth-grade education, a listening ear, a kitchen table, a Bible, and a coffeepot.

We believe that adding human care at this most basic level will be the most effective way to reach the goal of building a sustainable ministry of care. It is Romans 12:11-13 lived out: "Never be lacking in zeal, but keep your spiritual fervor, serving the Lord. Be joyful in hope, patient in affliction, faithful in prayer. Share with the Lord's people who are in need. Practice hospitality" (NIV).

We also believe that adding this basic level of care will better position the church to engage the broader community. Influential pastor and church leadership expert Carey Nieuwhof told us, "There are a growing number of initiatives right now to connect people who are lonely or in need with local churches. But many pastors simply don't have time to create the connection well. They may send an email back to the help seeker saying, 'Here are our service times—would love to see you on Sunday' but often don't have the capacity to go beyond that. And a church of three hundred may have only a few staff. So the pastors and staff need someone else in their church to reach out and text that person. The message is: You have lay people who can do this—use them!"[10]

As you can see in the depiction of the church CARE strategy, there is an additional crucial element that will allow this type of lay caregiving to make a real difference in a church like Pastor Brent's: a coordinator. Churches need a specialized helper to serve as a guide and adviser for the pastor and/or to filter people in need to the right level(s) of care. In many cases, this is a licensed counselor or trained coach who attends the church and volunteers for two or three hours a week, or a pastoral staff member with a counseling background who oversees the care ministry as part of their responsibilities. (The coordinator role will be explained in more detail in chapters 4 and 7.)

Enlisting the Aid of Mental Health Professionals

If you are a mental health professional or have helpful training (for example, as a coach or a medical professional), consider how you might be able to help your church respond to the need. You might be able to step into a coordinator role as the vital, final element in the suggested model. (For more on the need for professionals to work with churches in general, see *Beyond the Clinical Hour*.[11])

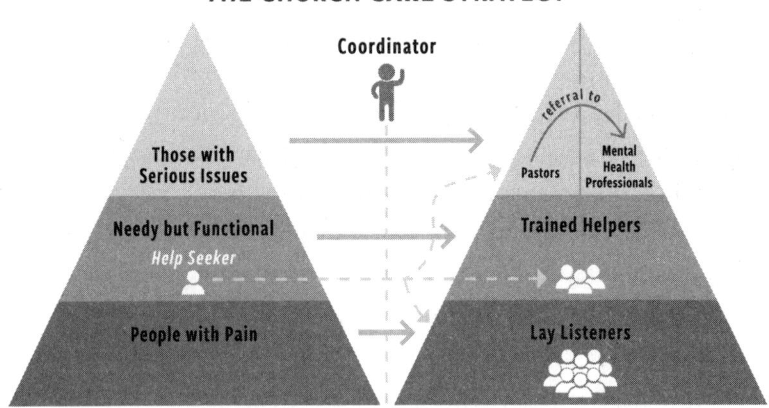

Every church has different needs and a unique culture, so it's important to lean in to whatever version of this is right for *you*. Some congregations might emphasize one area of the triangle more than the others, whether because of theology, resources, need, or capacity. But we believe that every leader must grapple with the truth that some form of this strategy is not a "nice to have"—it's a must-have.

The decisions for your church will be more complicated than a simple triangle. But with so many people experiencing mental health crises and so few helpers, it's essential for the church to step in as a source of human care—for people within the church and the culture as a whole.

Issue #2: People Feel Lonely, Isolated, and Abandoned

Beyond the first supply/demand reason for the pressure, the second phenomenon is a silent epidemic that impacts just about every aspect of life today: people are alone. Countless studies have found that relational connection is a prerequisite for human thriving—for mental, emotional, spiritual, relational, and even physical health—yet we live in a culture of significant isolation.[12]

This isolation is not from lack of desire for connection. According to a 2023 Pew study, 61 percent of adults believed that having close friends was "extremely or very important for people to live a fulfilling life.[13] Yet 15 percent of men had no close friends. Zero. That statistic has increased 500 percent in the past thirty years.[14]

This disconnection contributes to the mental health crisis and creates a barrier to solving it. Science confirms what we know from Scripture and from experience. As one researcher put it, "Friendships contribute to positive psychosocial adjustment in multiple domains, such as greater well-being, lower symptoms of depression, less delinquent and risky behaviors, and higher academic achievement; they also protect against the negative effects of victimization and internalizing behaviors."[15] We all need that person who will stick "closer than a brother" (Proverbs 18:24).

The bottom line is that people need friends. Real friends, not paid-professional friends, not just online friends (as helpful as they can be at times). We need real people who engage in real time over real concerns.

Here is where the church has an opportunity to show up. God designed us to live in the context of relationships (for example, see Genesis 2:18 and Hebrews 10:24-25). The power of Christian community and connection are key reasons why people who attend church regularly tend to be less lonely and have better marriages, physical health, and mental health.[16] But just because someone is in the church doesn't mean they are experiencing connection.

Solving the disconnection problem is essential for solving mental health in the church. In fact, we'd go so far as to say there's no way to have good mental health in the church without it.

Most church leaders agree. Eighty-six percent of those on our survey agreed that "a community of believers supporting one another is one of the best ways to foster good mental health inside the church." Less than 4 percent disagreed with that statement.

"A community of believers supporting one another is one of the best ways to foster good mental health inside the church."

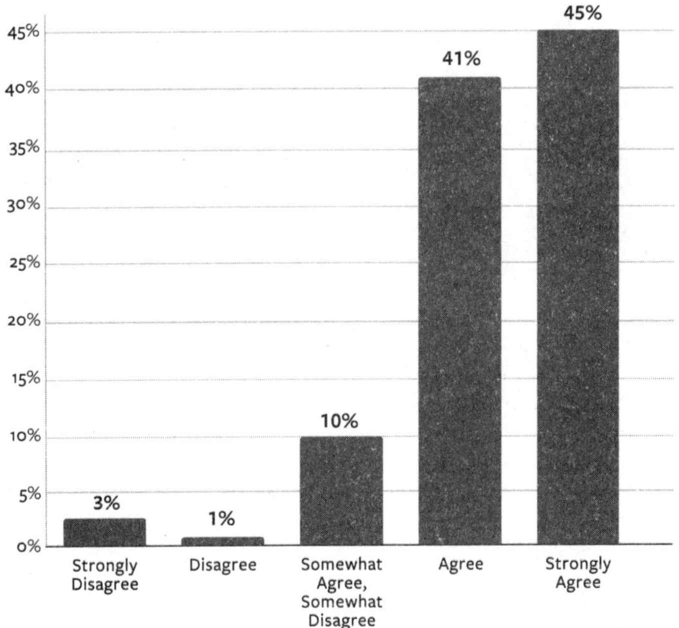

Let's look again at our triangles depicting the CARE strategy and how it can resolve not just the "traffic jam" problem but also the disconnection challenge. Pastors and professionals can't provide relational connection for everyone in their sphere, but the church can. Church care networks provide community, connections, and friendships that will help people become healthy and vibrant instead of lonely and struggling.

CARE: A SOLUTION FOR CONNECTION

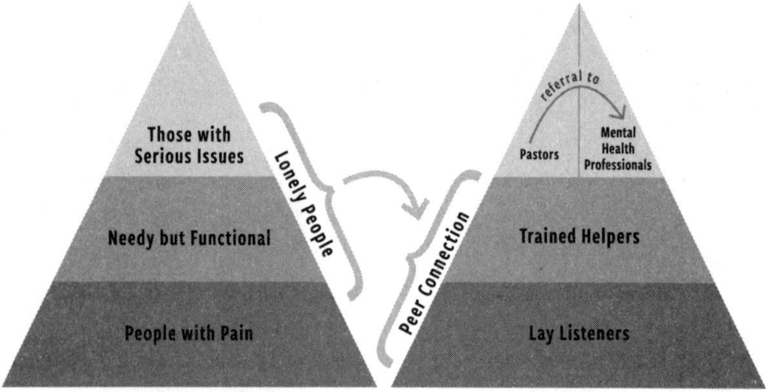

The CARE strategy is both prevention and cure. It is also, of course, what God has called us to all along: "God has given each of you a gift from his great variety of spiritual gifts. Use them well to serve one another. Do you have the gift of speaking? Then speak as though God himself were speaking through you. Do you have the gift of helping others? Do it with all the strength and energy that God supplies. Then everything you do will bring glory to God through Jesus Christ" (1 Peter 4:10-11, NLT).

Purposefully adding connection-oriented levels of care brings together the power of God and the power of His people. As David pondered the weight of his need, he wrote, "I keep my eyes always on the LORD. With him at my right hand, I will not be shaken" (Psalm 16:8, NIV). David's son Solomon understood both the weight and how it is lifted: "I saw the tears of the oppressed—and they have no comforter" (Ecclesiastes 4:1, NIV). The most effective and powerful treatment in addressing any kind of mental health suffering is the presence of a few close, committed, resilient, and steadfast friends. They humanize the gospel and declare its power.

Changing the Culture

We have a unique opportunity to shift the way we think of church outreach, human care, discipleship, and evangelism. In this model (which may seem new but is actually as old as the book of Acts), the church plays a central role in attending to human suffering. Our vision is for the church to step into its original design: to be the primary place where the love of God, redemption through Jesus, and the power of the Holy Spirit are experienced by the culture. Jesus' metaphors of salt and light suggest that we are to bring life to the world. Jesus entered into the culture by healing the leprous outcasts, giving sight to the blind, and restoring the woman at the well. In our day, we can bring comfort and healing to the isolated and lonely, help people see their great worth in God's eyes, and support the transformation of those in recovery.

For years, we have tended to think of mental health ministry as only being about helping people with specific, defined, and diagnosed disorders such as depression, anxiety, and personality disorders. Let's think bigger. Think of the church as the on-ramp through which people address their life pain. After all, much of the culture already does. According to a 2020 British study, "In America, as many as 40 percent seek support from clergy for mental health concerns, with studies identifying that individuals with mental health diagnoses were more likely to seek support from clergy alone, than psychiatrists and psychologists combined."[17]

Let's pause with that for a moment: these researchers, seeking ways to improve mental health services in the United Kingdom, looked "across the pond" and noted that for many in the US, the first step to obtaining mental health services is through the church. The church doesn't need to become the center of the solution; it already is. It just hasn't always realized or accepted this role.

As you'll see in chapter 3, our survey indicates that less than one-third of pastors (32 percent) had confidence that their church was "doing a good job addressing the mental health needs of our people." In other words, the Brits say that in the US, more people access the mental health system through the church than by contacting psychologists and psychiatrists combined. But we found that most pastors in the US say they don't address mental health needs well and could do it much better.

So we have the need, we have a culture with a near-desperate cry for aid, and we have a church capable of delivering the needed care as part of the great commission. It is here that need meets opportunity.

The Church Can Be the Solution

Mental health care is the evangelism, church growth, discipleship, and church engagement method of the twenty-first century. Rather than funneling people *out* of the church, we can view mental health as an opportunity to draw people in.

We increasingly hear pastors, church growth leaders, and clinicians calling for the church to lean in to this unique time in history. Christian psychiatrist and founder of Key Ministry Dr. Steve Grcevich says, "The church is faced with an enormous opportunity to present the gospel and engage with a vast population with untapped gifts and talents intended for the growth and edification of the church."[18]

Talbot School of Theology dean Ed Stetzer writes,

> Serving and saving were marks of Christ's life on earth. They should be marks of his people as well. But to do that, we must engage the broken and hurting people around us. I don't want to be part of a broken church—instead, I want to be a part of a church where broken people are welcome—a church where perfect people aren't allowed, a place where people can embark on this journey without having everything figured out from the start. That's hard. But it's what we were called to be. A church without the broken is a broken church.[19]

We have been here before—in a time of historic social crisis when the church showed up. During the Industrial Revolution in the late eighteenth and early nineteenth centuries, England endured a time of disease, darkness, and despair. Think of Dickens's *A Tale of Two Cities*: "The best of times . . . the worst of times." Most English children were illiterate, as were many of their parents, and most were also economically shackled to dreadful industry conditions. The prevailing philosophy of the day was work or starve; life was cheap; people could be replaced. Children worked in sweatshops, and there were no child labor laws, no public education. Schooling was a luxury, available only for wealthy children.

A publisher named Robert Raikes and Thomas Stock, the rector of Raikes's church, were disturbed by society's neglect of children and the deplorable life conditions of the working class. Seeing education as a way out of poverty, Raikes championed a radical idea: all children should learn to read—and the church should teach them.

Raikes and Stock considered their resources. They had Sundays, the one day when children were not at the factory. They had a church building. They had Christians who were willing to give their time. And they had a publishing company with the capacity to print books for curriculum.

With those resources—time, space, volunteers, and a tool—they taught kids. They called it Sunday school. Volunteers taught basic school skills, and they taught about Jesus.

The movement grew at a phenomenal rate. They went from schooling a handful of kids in 1780 to three hundred thousand children in less than ten years.[20] By the year 1850, there were more than two million children enrolled in Sunday school through the Church of England.[21]

It wasn't long before the movement took hold across Europe and the United States, among a wide range of denominations. Then in 1870, England passed the Elementary Education Act, taking what had begun in a few churches and formalizing a free public education system, which much of the world soon followed.[22]

Sunday schools changed the world. The church had created a new culture and brought great transformation during a time of great need.

Today, there is another massive human crisis—people are experiencing distress and isolation in proportions never seen. We have the tool: technology through which resources can be shared and scaled. We have a place: churches in every community. We have a plan: how churches can play a major role in addressing human care. And most importantly, we have a human resource: hundreds of thousands of ordinary people who are willing to care for others, many of whom want to be taught how to come alongside someone in pain.

The Next Creative Response Can Be Yours

The church is at an incredible crossroads right now. In every community, every denomination, every style and size of church, we see amazing, creative responses to the mental health crisis. There is a spontaneous response to a social need, with innovation and experimentation to answer the question "How can we do this well?"

The church is most effective at stepping forward into care ministry when it collaborates with existing mental health practices. It will not supplant or replace highly trained medical and therapeutic approaches. Nor will it replace pastoral counseling. Nor will it replace the vital and active ministries that have exploded over the last few decades. Rather, the effort will build on all of these, adding supportive, supervised volunteers who can serve the church as listeners, helpers, and disciple makers.

As you will see in the next chapter, there are churches who are already doing this well. Innovation is emerging. We hope to show you what others are doing so you can adapt the various ideas for the needs of your community and your church's DNA.

The key is to give people a way to get help in your church, even if you also refer to additional care. One concerned pastor and therapist put it this way:

> Many churches don't realize they are creating a perfect system to have people leave the church and look for help elsewhere. Now, of course, most churches can't hire a therapist or psychiatrist on staff. But what any church can do is create something that is lay-led. What any church can tell that person is, "We have something you can plug into immediately. Right now. As a church, we will refer you and help you see a counselor or psychiatrist if you need it. We're going to help you get connected to good community resources. But in the meantime, we have something right here."

2

Five Churches That Are Doing It Well

Creative Models from Others That Might Spark Your Own

A good example has twice the value of good advice.

ALBERT SCHWEITZER

Five different cities, five different leaders, five different churches. Each congregation has its own culture, its own priorities, its own demographics. But each of them has one thing in common: each recognized the mental health needs in their church and community, and decided to do something about it. Their *why* is the same: they all want to care for people well. They just differ on the *how*.

You may be convinced of the need for your church to fill in the gap and provide care for hurting people—and maybe even prevent some hurts as well. But you might not be sure how to go from knowing there's a need to knowing how to meet it.

In our survey of nearly 1,900 pastors, church leaders, and mental health professionals, we asked, "What is the one most important thing you would want to ask another leader who has already created a robust mental health ministry effort in their church?" Sixty percent of the pastors responded, and by far their top question was: *How?* Specifically, "How do we do this mental health thing in our church? What does it look like? How did you get started?"

We're guessing you may have those same questions.

We will be answering them in more detail in the coming chapters. To begin, following Schweitzer's suggestion, we'll share five true stories of churches from a variety of styles, cultures, ethnicities, and sizes that are doing this well—and doing it very differently.[1] We hope these examples will stir creativity and help you assess what might work in your community, garner resources, and make plans.

Think of these as archetypes—models to help churches with similar philosophies or needs:

- There's the rural church whose leaders wanted to help their people in an area with few mental health professionals and ended up creating a vibrant Friday-night ministry.
- There's the large church with a licensed clinical social worker in the congregation that built up a robust program of dozens of trained lay counselors, thereby helping hundreds more people than could be seen by licensed professionals.
- There's the small church whose pastor wondered how to help his people with a small budget and a limited team, then created a culture of openness and got creative with resources both inside and outside his church.
- There's the church with a strong philosophy toward biblical counseling whose ministry of trained, certified biblical

counselors, medical professionals, and pastors not only helps those in their church but also trains others across their region.
- And there's the church with the philosophy that counseling should come only from licensed professionals, which created a way to refer out while also walking alongside those in need.

While single models are helpful, they can take us only so far. As many pastors told us, every church has its own DNA, and leaders need ideas and processes that work for them. So in the next few chapters, we share various ideas as sidebars—helpful or creative concepts that work for different churches. All of these point toward the same CARE strategy goal of involving people at all levels of the church to meet all levels of need. Think of these as building blocks that you can mix, match, and merge with your own unique approaches to create something that is right for you and the people you serve.

As you read the following case studies, you'll notice that although many of the processes are different, the needs and concerns (and some of the creative ideas) apply to every type and size of church, as well as to any pastor or church leader.

The Recovery Church

Community Church (not its real name[2]) sits in a prominent spot in a quiet town about an hour's drive from the nearest small city. Beyond the church building, forests and farmlands fill the horizon. Like roughly a third of those living in the United States, those in this community are in a mental health desert, or what the government calls a mental health workforce shortage area.[3] There aren't nearly enough caregivers. Unmet needs abound in the church and the community—and the pastors feel it.

Community Church had limited options. If a couple was on the verge of divorce, if someone faced an addiction, or if a teenager was questioning their gender identity, pastors—several of whom juggled other part-time jobs—could see people for a few sessions. But they didn't have the capacity or the training to truly meet the need. They referred out to mental health professionals, knowing that the waiting lists often extended to three or four months. Some people in need might be able to find a telehealth professional or a professional in the city, but it was hard for pastors to evaluate the trustworthiness of services from such a distance.

Even if a church member could get in to see a mental health professional, the cost was often prohibitive. The church used its benevolence fund to subsidize professional services, but many people couldn't afford it, even at a reduced cost.

The breaking point came when a pastor saw a church member who was struggling with an addiction. This person was doing everything the pastor advised—going to Bible studies, meeting with an accountability group, and being discipled—but still couldn't get control of his life. The pastor recognized that this was just one story among many. The realization came: *there has to be a way to get all these people more specific help*.

The church had been saving money to renovate their old sanctuary. The pastor told his board that they needed to use that money for a part-time position instead and see if they could start something to help with a mental health and recovery ministry—perhaps even a program that would bring new people into the church and pay for itself over time.

The board agreed, and they hired a licensed mental health professional/pastor who had been part of leading a popular recovery program at a church in another state. He got to work and built a new model: a "come as you are" Friday night with dinner and fellowship, worship, and discussion, as well as midweek small groups—all based on a Christian twelve-step program.

Why a twelve-step program, when the issues were broader than traditional addiction and recovery? The pastor/clinician offered two key reasons.

> First, recovery is not defined by a singular issue like drugs and alcohol. Recovery is defined by a *process* that works with just about any issue. And that's me as a licensed clinical social worker saying this. I've used this process with folks who are struggling with deep depression, relationship issues, anxiety, pornography, borderline personality, bipolar—you name it. As people get connected to the twelve steps, it brings a tremendous amount of healing.

> Second, and just as important:

> What recovery programs can do is give the church a very important in-house option. What most pastors or mental health coach positions will do—and this is often appropriate—is recognize that a need is greater than they

> can meet and refer *out* of the church. But because we're overwhelmed in the counseling world, with waiting lists months long, that's not going to work for people who are in crisis. So the church needs in-house options while they are waiting. As the church, we don't want to be saying, "God can't help you, but the world can."

The core of this program became connection with others. The church believed that, as the saying goes, "The opposite of addiction is not sobriety. The opposite of addiction is connection." The pastor pointed out, "In all areas, people recover when they get connected to safe and supportive, healthy folks."

The church began offering a community dinner each Friday night as the entry point to a simple program with food and fellowship, worship, a testimony, a short lesson, and a group discussion. During the week, everyone participated in small groups to share, listen, and learn. Word began to spread. Just a few years later, Community Church has four hundred to five hundred people flooding the building every Friday night.

The church has found that many of those individuals begin coming on Sunday morning as well, plugging in to the life of the church and becoming helpers in their turn. The pastor/clinician told us:

> We find that churches love recovery programs, because they turn pew sitters into soul winners. People start telling others, "Let me tell you about my Jesus and what He did for me." They get so excited. They want to serve. You can't keep them out of the church. They want to get in there and help other people.

Something else interesting began to happen:

> Somewhere along the way, the people on the waiting lists for professional counseling often say, "You know what? I think I'm good. I'm working my program; I'm connected to really good, safe, supportive people; I'm serving in the church. I feel like I have purpose. I feel loved. I feel the power of God working in me. I think I'm good for now." It's amazing how often that happens. And it all happened *inside* the church, not outside the church.

It all happened inside the church, not outside the church. Community Church shows us that a fairly simple model can transform a church and a community.

The Lay Counseling Church

Ten years ago, a pastor at City Church, a congregation with 1,500 members in a populous metro area, had a revelation: many of the people he was referring to mental health professionals really didn't need such a high level of care. A free lay counseling program would help many people with basic and mid-level needs, and it would also free up professionals to see those who needed more support. The pastor hired Luke, a church member who was a licensed clinical social worker, as a contractor to run the program for ten hours a week.

Ten years later, the program—and the church—is thriving, with thirty volunteer lay counselors. They have a robust system for intake, training, and supervision, as well as downtime when a lay counselor needs a break between clients, and a careful process for referrals. Each volunteer sees a client for a maximum of ten sessions. These volunteers conduct more than one thousand hours of basic counseling each year, resulting in countless lives changed in the church and the broader community.

The counseling center is on-site at the church. There's a clear separation from the church to protect confidentiality. Clients enter a designated door, and lay counselors do not share private details with others. The church refers the help seekers to lay counselors, and the lay counselors refer help seekers to small groups and other avenues so they can plug in to the life of the church.

As Luke explained, "For example, the church has a GriefShare group. If someone finds their individual journey is bigger than that, they are referred to lay counseling. Or if someone in lay counseling is dealing with grief but has never been part of GriefShare, we might recommend that they plug in there during and after counseling."

People who are likely to make good lay counselors (LCs) are recommended by one of the pastors and vetted during the training. They begin an eleven-week training session, where they learn a simplified, biblically focused version of cognitive behavioral therapy (CBT). As many pastors and Christian therapists have noted, CBT emphasizes what we allow ourselves to "think on" and believe, and what we feel and do as a result. Thus, it includes many elements that are consistent with biblical teaching, such as Philippians 4:6-8. Luke explained:

> What I have done is make the training simple for the LCs. They don't go in depth, but it's integrated. This is beyond a

> ministry like Stephen Ministries that is primarily mentoring. The LCs are actually given some specific mental health knowledge and do things like role-playing in their training. But they're not getting a professional degree in this. I have teachers, I have nurses, I have retirees. So I reduced the CBT process down to three questions. There are multiple models of these questions. But I use three.
>
> First, the LC helps the distressed client consider, "Is my thinking based on fact?" Second, "Is my thinking helping me feel the way I want to feel?" And third, "Is my thinking helping me reach a goal or expectation?" So that's a little mini-tool you can give to somebody when they're stuck, when they're struggling. They can challenge their own perceptions of an event and maybe pick a different way to go.

One of the lay counselors, Leslie, described how this often plays out with her clients:

> I lean on Philippians 4:8, about how to fix our thoughts: "If anything is excellent or praiseworthy—think about such things." So we can ask the person, "Okay, how are *you* thinking?" The basic grid of CBT that we are urged to ask is, "Is this thought you're having true and based on fact?" Is it really true that your husband is working so much because he no longer cares about you? Then, "Is this thought helping you feel the way you want to feel? And is it helping you get where you want to go?"

> If the answer to any of those questions is no, their thoughts aren't serving them well. And suddenly they realize, "I have agency. I may not be able to fix this problem on my own, but I can fix my thoughts!" That is when the dominoes start to fall. That is the gatekeeper to all of it. And then we pivot to the future: "Okay, what can you do instead? What can you think and do now that will build a healthy life?"

The lay counselors are asked to make a one-year commitment and attend mandatory monthly supervision meetings with Luke. Many church-led lay counseling programs have a similar requirement for monthly meetings. "A structure like that *has* to be in place for this type of thing to work," Luke said. "Being a greeter or running the coffee bar or working in the nursery is awesome, but this is a different type of ministry."

So how do people enter the system? When a person calls or emails the church, they are first funneled to the church's part-time counseling center administrator (the only actual church employee in the program). They fill out a detailed intake form with their contact information, demographics, and answers to questions about their current concern and situation. Luke reviews the intakes and determines who is a fit. When the person's need goes beyond the LC's training—for example, if the person is actively using substances or is considering self-harm—they are redirected to a mental health professional.

An important task for every ministry is to develop an intake form. There are many examples online, including at Thechurchcares.com. See the sidebar for some sample items that might appear on such a form.

Sample of a Partial (Not Comprehensive) Intake Form

[Note: This is possible wording on an intake form.]

To help us evaluate your need, please complete the following questions. Be assured that the information will be kept confidential, seen only by those who will help make placement decisions. You will receive an initial phone intake from the ministry to understand your needs. This form will serve as a starting place for that conversation. **If you need to speak with someone immediately, please call the emergency number 911 or the mental health emergency number 988.**

[Note: These are sample questions. The full intake form might include other items.]

- What concerns led you to contact the church?
- When did the concerns begin?
- What church do you attend?
- How often do you attend?
- Briefly describe your relationship with God.
- Are you concerned about your current drug or alcohol use and amounts? Yes/No (If yes, please explain.)
- Are you currently experiencing any physical complications (e.g., headaches, body aches, or stomach problems)? Yes/No (If yes, please explain.)
- Have you had previous experience in counseling? Yes/No (If yes, describe reason for counseling, dates, and counselor's contact information.)
- Either recently or in the past, have you had suicidal thoughts? Yes/No
- Either recently or in the past, have you made suicide attempts or attempted acts of self-harm? Yes/No
- What actions have you taken to deal with this situation (e.g., small group, support group)?
- What would you like to accomplish or gain from your sessions with the counseling ministry?

When the person is a candidate for lay counseling, an LC is approached. Jon, one LC, said he's asked, "Here's what is going on with this person—are you ready to take it?" He explained, "We don't take on clients until we're in a space to do so. Having permission to take care of ourselves too is a really big deal." During the intake and during the first meeting, those who come in for lay counseling acknowledge that this isn't the same as professional counseling; the volunteers are there for basic listening, help, and support.

Another LC said, "People will often come in and say, 'What should I do? What do you think?' Every time I say, 'That's not what we're here for. We're taking this drive together, but my job is to put *you* in the driver's seat.'"

Most churches with effective lay counseling programs find that a culture of openness is essential. Manny, another LC, put it this way: "As people walk onto the church campus, they need to know that they are in a judgment-free zone rather than a judgment zone. People are looking for love. But if I can judge you, then I have a reason not to love you. These programs work so well because we are committed to an overall culture of open arms and acceptance."

The Small-Size, Large-Impact Church

Pastor Ross grew up not far away from Family Church, where his uncle was the pastor and where he is now at the helm. About a hundred people attend the service on any given Sunday, with roughly half that number attending on Wednesday nights. The core of the church is made up of several involved families of multiple generations, including many single mothers and their kids.

Historically, the approach to mental health issues in this church was silence: "Nothing to see here." He emphasizes that this wasn't from a lack of care but from a lack of knowledge and comfort with the topic.

But Pastor Ross was different, having gone through mental health struggles and psychiatric treatment himself. As a veteran, he was treated for PTSD and anxiety, and he saw firsthand how his church and others needed to grapple with the issue.

> When I was going through all my situations and struggles, I saw the looks I got and the way I was treated from the pew and other leaders. It was important to me to do something—not just for people in our church, but also for the other people we impact. I do some chaplain work for the local hospital and for first responders, and there's a lot of need there too.

Like most small church pastors, Ross didn't have extra money or time. But there were three things he could change. First, to help with both prevention and necessary treatment, he wanted to change the Family Church culture and make it okay to talk about mental health instead of hiding behind a "nothing to see here" mask.

> I started being transparent. My wife always tells me, "You are more effective when you talk about *you*." I'm not afraid to say I've been there. I've been to counseling. I've had PTSD, and childhood trauma. I say from the pulpit that both my wife and I have gone to see professionals. If I can see a professional heart surgeon, I can see a professional for other issues of the heart. I model what needs to happen.

> People are now drawn to this church, and drawn to share, because I say I've been dinged and dented and suffered.

His second effort was to build organic internal support:

> We can't talk about everything, every Sunday, from the stage. So let's also bring it down to the small group level. In some cases, we've had everyone go through a specific curriculum. But mostly we ask people to just talk about it. Loneliness. Insecurities. Lack of belonging.
>
> One of the only ways to do that is by building a greater sense of community. For example, we had people start group text threads for each small group. People stay connected that way, and ask for prayer, and share what is going on. We also asked the groups to do something together socially once a month or so.

Pastor Ross asked a few trusted volunteers to mentor people who needed care and support. That freed him up to do more pastoral counseling with those who needed it most. Sometimes those trusted volunteers were people who had gone through something challenging themselves, which created a positive cycle. Ross told us, "As we do this, we have more people come to the altar and be helped because we are bringing the people who have gone through it and *can* help."

Third, Pastor Ross began to build up the church's external resources. He needed relationships with more professionals in private practice so he could refer people to them. He also needed ways to help people pay for it. He especially needed options *other* than professional counseling—other ways external resources could equip people in the church.

He asked trusted church members to help him look into local resources and develop relationships. They worked on this for a year. They met with social workers, county government liaisons, first-responder agencies, a hospital, several schools, a regional inpatient program for those with eating disorders, and nonprofit foundations that were willing to contribute financially toward mental health services. The goal was to build relationships they could turn to for help, advice, or equipping when it was needed.

> I realized I had a friend who works at the children's hospital who connected me with a helpful children's psychiatrist there. He was willing to be an ally and be available to provide some informal guidance if kids were involved. Particularly if there was abuse, ADHD issues—that sort of thing. He'll talk with me briefly or send me an email and say, "Here's what I informally recommend," and I forward that content to the family.
>
> We also asked the director of the local counseling center to conduct a community seminar on mental health at the church. So many people came that we're doing them regularly now.

As an unexpected benefit, the relationships began to go both ways. Pastor Ross offered his services as a chaplain to the police and fire departments:

> I'm able to serve the county by working with first responders. I refer some of these people to a mental health specialist, and she's certainly willing to work with them. But usually a cop will want to talk to me, not her, because he doesn't want it on his record. First responders will talk to a pastor, priest, chaplain—but often avoid professionals.

Pastor Ross summarized his advice for the small church this way: "Pastors can use so many resources in the community. If you don't have it in the church, it's in the community you serve. Your hospital, your nonprofits, your government, other churches have it. The help is there."

The Biblical Counseling Church

More than forty years ago, several ministry friends started a small biblical counseling center in a church basement. The group included the pastor of the church (Legacy Church), a seminary student, and a medical doctor who were all working together to create a counseling program. They saw people on Mondays, free of charge. Pastor Scott, the current pastor of Legacy Church, told us, "It wasn't all that sophisticated, but the slots filled up quickly. Then they started not only counseling people but training people. And people started coming in the doors."

Fast-forward to today:

> Legacy Church has grown to several thousand people and has counseling centers at our various campuses. On a typical

> Monday, there are about thirty of us—most of our pastoral staff, a number of medical doctors, and some other godly women and men who have been trained and certified. We serve our church members throughout the week, and on Mondays we make biblical counseling services available to hundreds or thousands of people in our community each year, free of charge. And we train hundreds more who take that training back to their church and begin similar ministries. Having this center has positioned us as a place that cares about people who are hurting. And that's what we want to be known for.

What happened over those forty years to result in such a remarkable outcome? Pastor Scott's answer is just as much about the biblical counseling philosophy as it is about a counseling process:

> We believe that biblical counseling is a part of the church accomplishing the great commission. But most people really don't know what biblical counseling is. We live in a therapeutic culture and most people don't even know there's another option.
>
> Basically, if it's a nonmedical issue, biblical counselors believe that we find everything we need to know about life and godliness on the pages of Scripture. We are doing soul care. We don't agree that to really hear the deep problems of human beings we must have the findings of secular psychology. It's not that those findings are usually bad, but

> we believe they don't necessarily get at the real issues under the psychological descriptions.
>
> Of course, sometimes the issues *are* medical issues, which is why, from the very beginning, we have worked hand in hand with medical doctors. We want to look at proven medical science and be careful about what's happening in someone's life physiologically as well.

To follow up, we asked, "How does a biblical counseling approach work, compared to a more standard counseling approach?" Pastor Scott provided a helpful example:

> We were working with a young twentysomething man with OCD who was in great distress. Until we dug into what was going on in the heart, he didn't realize what was really under his compulsive behaviors. It turns out, they were a subconscious attempt to atone for something: he was ashamed of sexual thoughts he was having about women he knew. He didn't think of it as self-atonement or as rejecting what Jesus had already done for him, but that's what he was doing. And he was in the grip of fear and hopelessness as a result. As we worked together, once he began to truly grasp what God had done for him and in him through Jesus and once he learned how to bring those fears to God in a practical way, he began to change naturally.
>
> That is often the way it works. It's a process. The person begins to use biblical tools, like taking destructive

> desires and thoughts captive and building godly desires and thoughts in their place. And much of that may not even be touched on if the person was sitting with a secular professional who started with exposure therapy, for example.
>
> We want to provide a level of depth but in a way that's consistent with theological truths, biblical truths. And since we're going to the real issues, people get really helped.

To avoid slipping into a reductionistic approach ("Take two prayers and call me in the morning"), Legacy Church places an emphasis on training, taking volunteers through an apprenticeship and certification program. "People come for eleven consecutive Mondays. They receive a lecture in the morning and then sit in on live counseling sessions." They're trained to focus on the core of biblical counseling, which is looking at matters of the heart—including their own.

> We believe the Bible has a very robust theology of the heart. That's what biblical counseling is really focused on. Let's name the real issue we're talking about and let's get beyond behavior, to what is going on in the nuances of our hearts. And thankfully, redemption can change what is going on at the level of the heart.
>
> Biblical counseling resources are getting richer by the year, so it works in making disciples in local churches, and it works in reaching our communities for Christ.

As the reach of the counseling center grew, so did interest from the community.

> Our community knows that we provide robust biblical counseling resources that are changing lives and therefore changing the community, so they don't view us as being simplistic or unscientific. We end up working closely with a lot of mental health providers.
>
> Many times, a mental health provider will have a client say, "I wonder if this issue has something to do with my relationship with God." And that mental health provider pretty quickly says, "It may, but that's not my bailiwick. It *is* Legacy's, though." So the provider refers them to us. We don't approach matters of the heart the same way as the secular mental health world, but we don't have to develop some sort of an adversarial relationship. They know we're different. But in this day and age, there's much more of an openness. In part because it works, and in part because people are asking for it.

The Church That Refers Out—and Walks Alongside

Pastors Calvin and Jeanne, a married pastoral couple, moved into a metro area where a lot of industry was moving out. They planted Connection Church, and ten years later, the church is growing and attracting people of all different socioeconomic and educational backgrounds and mental health needs.

As part of their master plan for their church, they sought to create a community counseling center. But they quickly discovered that the restrictions and entanglements in their state were burdensome.

> We wanted to use only licensed clinicians, as we've had to unwind problems caused by unprepared, unlicensed counselors in the past. But we also needed to be able to counsel everyone we saw from a biblical point of view rather than having to affirm certain secular views that we view as damaging, such as those on sexuality or abortion. And using licensed therapists meant billing insurance because so many people in our area use Medicaid. But the rules and red tape in our area just made all that a challenge.

Because of the significant challenges, they pivoted to a different model. Rather than create an in-house ministry, they partnered with Christian clinicians.

> We just had to work hard to establish relationships with professionals who were available to us for a certain number of hours and who we could trust in the same way we would trust someone in-house. But just as important, we needed some way to ensure that the people who needed help were actually getting it. And we needed some sort of pathway for ongoing care for them within the church at the same time. So that meant engaging volunteer lay leaders.
>
> The core of what we wanted to do was to have a mental health solution from professionals—but one that was part

of this discipleship pathway in the church. So we built a process based on what we call our "mental health advocates."

Pastor Jeanne coordinates the ministry and the advocates. She said,

> Think of the advocates as a sort of a mental health concierge. The advocates walk with you to get you to where you can be restored. They do all sorts of things *except* counseling. They will listen to what your need is and refer you to a list of several resources outside and inside the church. Then they will check in with you and ask, "Have you called that therapist yet to get on the waiting list?"
>
> Or if the answer is no, "Why not? What can I do to turn that no into a yes?" So they troubleshoot and help remove obstacles to care. Like, if you're a single mom who has no one to watch the kids so you can actually go to counseling, the advocate will babysit or find a babysitter.
>
> Just as important, they try to get you to ongoing support within the church. We might refer that single mom to a therapist, but we are also going to refer her to internal resources: "Let me connect you to our MomCo group for moms of young kids."

Advocates are chosen and trained carefully. They are seen as an extension of the pastoral staff, reporting back to the pastoral team with the unique needs and challenges people are facing so the church doesn't lose track of those who have been referred out.

Pastor Calvin summarized the ministry with this conclusion:

> With the advocates, we're able to expand our load and the number of people we help. And it builds a great impression of the church as loving people due to adding that kind of white-glove service. Jeanne does a great job reminding the advocates that even though this is a mental health ministry, we're not in the counseling business. We teach the advocates to love, talk, listen, understand, validate, empathize, and give those referrals. They pray with them, maybe they meet them for coffee, maybe they meet them here at the church and take them to a grief support group or whatever it may be. And they keep doing that, even after the person is successfully in counseling, if they need it. The key is: we're coming alongside, to make the whole process a little less overwhelming, and get them some social support and follow-up.

The Caring Church in Many Shapes, Sizes, and Shades

We've interviewed more than one hundred Christian leaders who are effectively leaning into the church being a light in the mental health crisis. We've seen examples from hundreds more. While it may seem like a big "lift" to get an effective mental health ministry off the ground, most churches are more innovative, motivated, and organized than they realize. Indeed, we heard that reassurance from multiple pastors and church leaders who are already engaged in this kind of ministry. It requires a church to be purposeful, not perfect.

These five stories represent broadly different approaches. The sidebars in the chapters that follow offer a host of other bite-sized, creative ideas from churches with effective programs. Think of these as highlights in a travel guide: they can illuminate possibilities, help you figure out where you might want to go, and get you started on the journey. Examples can indeed be more valuable than advice.

You might be wondering, *What sort of journey are other pastors and church leaders taking? What mental health ministries are happening in other churches? Am I the only one who has a hidden concern about certain obstacles?*

We had these questions and many more—so we asked. In chapter 3, we share the outcomes of our national survey of pastors and church leaders regarding how mental health concerns are understood and addressed in the church today. As you will see, if you're asking these questions, you're not alone. There are many people trying to figure this out, and there's much to learn from them.

3

The State of the Church

Identifying Current Trends and Perspectives Around Mental Health

---

Know from whence you came. If you know whence you came, there are absolutely no limitations to where you can go.

JAMES BALDWIN

When I (Jim) am with my two-year-old granddaughter, I do my part to pass on the really important things in life. Which of course includes the classic rhyme and hand motions:

Here is the church.
    Here is the steeple.
Open the doors, and see all the people.

When I showed her this the other day, she asked to see it again. And again. (Any parent or grandparent knows the drill.) It's a simple rhyme, but I was struck that this threefold framework is behind a lot of what we're talking about when it comes to human care.

This chapter focuses on the state of the church when it comes to mental health efforts, the role of the steeple, and the needs of the people. The church is where care happens. The steeple is how the church presents itself to the community—the visible declaration of "Here we are; we can help!" The people are both the ones who need healing and those who provide the healing. Even today, in our "post-Christian" culture, with all the failings of an institution made up of imperfect humans, the church remains a trusted and reliable place for people in need—which is all of us. We all need redemption, reconciliation, discipleship, fellowship, and a listening ear. In each of these areas, church steeples—whether physical or metaphorical—remain a visible marker to those inside and outside the church walls.

After all, the committed followers of Jesus who regularly go to church (about 30 percent of the US population),[1] *are* the church. When I (Shaunti) was getting my master's degree at Harvard, my pastor (himself a Harvard grad) conducted services for students and community members in a campus building and worked out of a separate office. One day a tax assessor showed up at the tiny office for a snap inspection. He looked around and said suspiciously, "Where's the church?" Our pastor said he was legitimately confused for a minute. He answered, in a puzzled voice, "Well, some of them are at work, some of them are at school . . ."

That view of the church is, of course, the biblical one. This is what the CARE model is based on: mobilizing the church to meet the needs of the church and the community.

To understand the current perspectives among leaders about the role of the church, the steeple (how the church presents itself to the community), and the people in meeting today's mental, emotional, and relational needs, we interviewed and surveyed more than two thousand pastors, church leaders, and mental health professionals. Several clear trends emerged. Think of this chapter as a state of the church briefing—a tour of the most common and important views and actions around mental health in the church today.

Understanding—and Using—the Data

Understanding the trends isn't just important because we should know the state of the church today, although that's part of it, but also because this can help us think through our own perspective and strategies.

You might find it helpful to use the points in this chapter as an initial informal assessment for your church and ministry perspective. How are you already seizing some of these opportunities? Do you hold any perceptions that contradict one another? Which obstacles need to be overcome, and how might you do that?

We hope you will read this chapter with a pen in hand and make notes as you go.

Before we dive in, we do want to share a few basic details about the data, which was rigorously gathered and represents as broad of a view as we could arrange.

For the anonymous survey, we partnered with multiple organizations across many streams of the church, each of which sent a unique survey link to their pastors or other leaders. These partners included multiple denominations, ministries, and Christian mental health groups across the theological, ethnic, and cultural spectrum. We purposefully sought input from Protestants and Catholics; progressives and conservatives; churches with rich, well-planned liturgies and those with highly flexible, led-by-the-Spirit approaches; churches with one predominant ethnic group (e.g., Black, white, or Hispanic) and those that were culturally blended. We created a Spanish-language version of the survey for several partner groups. The survey encompassed input from megachurches, large churches, midsize churches, small churches, and house churches.

Survey participants were clergy, church staff, ministry leaders, counselors, or other leaders who work extensively in or with the church. In total, 1,852 leaders participated in English, and 36 in Spanish. Two-thirds (66 percent) of participants were pastors, priests, or bishops.[2] (As noted in chapter 1, we are referring to all clergy as pastors.)

Roughly 20 percent of respondents were church staff or ministry directors, involved pastors' spouses, governing elders, parish council members, active volunteers, or other similar roles. Fourteen percent were mental health professionals or in a wide array of other roles, such as chaplains, diocese coordinators, or denominational leaders.

In addition to the national survey, we conducted hundreds of research interviews and other conversations with a diverse group of leaders. All told, the data below is drawn from well over two thousand pastors and church leaders.

Ten Trends in the Church

Dozens of trends emerged from the data. We will focus on ten that we believe will be most helpful. As you consider each theme, we invite you to ask, *What about me? What about my church? What about my community?*

Trend #1: Most pastors see the mental health needs but say their church isn't effective in addressing them yet.

Half of church leaders agree that mental health issues are common in their church, with the number rising to 81 percent when including those who somewhat agree. A total of 19 percent believed mental concerns are not common.

While most acknowledge that the need exists, pastors' perceptions of how well the need is being met can be split into thirds. About one-third believe that mental health needs are being met in the church. A little less than a third are confident that their church is *not* doing a good job. And a little more than a third are not sure—they see their church as good in some areas, not so good in others. The reasons given for lack of effective ministry were all over the map but often stemmed from a simple lack of capacity and/or the fear of a pastor or layperson "messing someone up." (Both issues will be addressed in chapter 5.)

"Our church has an effective process in place; we are doing a good job of addressing the mental health needs of our people."

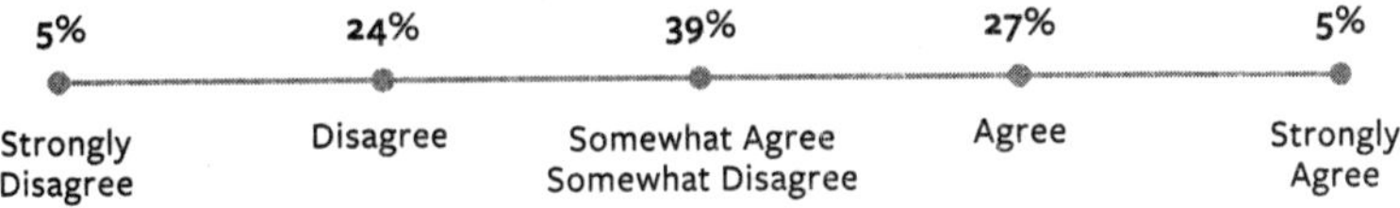

Thankfully, where churches are willing to purposefully address mental health concerns, the congregation is likely to be supportive. The shame around discussing mental health in the church, which was common in previous generations, has greatly diminished. While that stigma certainly exists in individual church cultures—11 percent of pastors thought the stigma remained high—70 percent disagreed that there is any stigma today, with 20 percent being on the fence. Two-thirds of churches affirmed, "In my church, being in counseling is seen in a favorable light," with the ratio rising to 95 percent when including those who somewhat agreed.

Low Stigma Around Mental Health in the Church

	Disagree	Somewhat agree/ Somewhat disagree	Agree
"In my church, seeing a therapist for emotional and interpersonal problems carries social stigma."	70%	20%	11%
"People in my church will see a person in a less favorable way if they come to know that he/she has seen a therapist."	79%	17%	5%
"In my church, being in counseling is seen in a favorable light."	6%	29%	66%
Note: Percentages do not equal 100% due to rounding.			

In the interviews, many pastors said that when they talk about mental health, people respond. This makes it much easier to develop a mental health ministry. As one explained, "When we said we wanted to explore this area of ministry, the response was huge. And for those who are tentative, we say from the stage that therapy and Jesus are not in competition or in conflict with each other. Just as He has given us the ability to navigate knee replacements, He's given us wisdom for rewiring the brain via therapy and conversation and, if you need it, prescription medication."

Although there's still work to be done to bring openness to these issues and there will always be differences of opinion on how to address them, it's encouraging that much of what used to be hidden in the shadows around mental health is being brought into the light.

Trend #2: Whether a pastor feels overwhelmed by the need is directly related to their personal interaction with the need.

The pastors who saw the need were overwhelmed by it. Among church leaders who saw mental health issues as common, 75 percent thought that "addressing the mental health needs of the congregation has contributed to the pastor(s) in our church being overworked."[3] Almost all of those (94 percent) agreed that it was "greater than I can address alone."

For pastors who didn't see it as a major issue, 31 percent agreed or somewhat agreed that it contributed to them being overworked, and just 41 percent said the need was greater than they could address alone.

"The current mental health need in my church is greater than I can address alone."

	Disagree	Somewhat agree/ Somewhat disagree	Agree
Those who believe mental health issues are common	6%	11%	83%
Those who believe mental health issues are not common	59%	25%	16%

Now, maybe mental health issues are not as common in some churches, or perhaps certain churches excel at preventing those concerns. But those two reasons are unlikely to explain why so many leaders (19 percent) believe mental health issues are not common, given the prevalence of these issues across all demographic groups (and given that those leaders were just as likely as any other leader to say they had—or did not have—an effective mental health process in their church).

An important finding was that senior pastors—who, in addition to being shepherds, also run the church, attend meetings, prepare sermons, and solve crises—may be less aware of the prevalence of need than other pastors or members of their staff. Senior pastors were significantly more likely to say that mental health issues were not common compared to those with other responsibilities in the church.

How prevalent are mental health issues in the congregation? The view by ministry role.

Primary ministry role in the church	Senior pastor	Other pastor	Ministry director	Licensed mental health professional
Believe mental health issues are common	46%	63%	66%	68%
Believe mental health issues are not common	23%	13%	5%	2%
Note: This is not a full list of roles in the church. Columns do not total 100% because the middle group (those who answered "somewhat agree/somewhat disagree") is not included.				

Pastors who think mental health issues are common are far more likely to consider themselves experienced and trained in dealing with those issues (42 percent) than to consider themselves not experienced (19 percent). We see what we are trained to see, and we tend not to recognize what we have less experience in.

As one pastor noted on the survey, "After the tragic loss of a staff member to suicide, we developed a mental health wellness plan for our staff. I highly recommend this for every church."

Now, to start sharing the ideas we mentioned, let's look at our first sidebar.

IDEA: On-Duty Volunteers at Worship Services

In many churches, a simple but highly effective ministry is to have a mental health minister "on duty" and available every week during and after worship services, drawn from a team of trained laypeople, mental health professionals, or other caregivers. As one leader described about a particular church: "They have the red chair, where nurses and paramedics sit, and it is always staffed. Everyone knows that if you trip and fall, that's where you go. They have the green chair, and this is where the mental health coaches sit. When someone is in the bathroom crying, everyone is trained to spot it and goes and gets the coach. The coach sits with them and starts the dialogue."

Trend #3: Pastors are torn about the consequences of referring out because of the scarcity of Christian professionals, too high a cost, and a risk of damaging advice.

As discussed in chapter 1, most pastors see referring out as what they "should" do. Yet many pastors are also torn about certain consequences of doing so.

One pastor captured the three most common concerns we heard: a dearth of Christian counselors, the cost, and the risk that the counselor will not guide the counselee well.

> If it's beyond my scope, we look to refer. But the referral stage is often when we have trouble. We don't have a large network of people we feel confident with in the counseling industry. There just aren't many Christian professionals here. Also, an immediate thing that comes up is the issue of cost. So few counselors take insurance, and people have to pay out of pocket. So how many sessions can they really do with that counselor, you know?
>
> Then there's the whole question of where the counselor stands with some of the cultural questions, the biblical questions. There's an organization in our area that says they provide Christian counseling, and it's really Christian in name only. When it comes to questions of Christian sexual ethics, they're not operating on any kind of guideline that comes through Scripture.

This pastor referenced a teenage girl in his congregation who was questioning her gender identity.

> When you're putting this child in the hands of someone who is not a Christian at all, they will hopefully address some of the things that are compounding the issues—like anxiety or other things. But there will not be any talking about how God made you and He loves you as you are. Or how this girl is processing her feelings with God in the midst of all of this. Or the potential spiritual issues underneath. Those things really matter, but they won't be addressed. Or if they are, it could be in the wrong direction.

The desire to have trustworthy counsel is why 71 percent of pastors agreed or somewhat agreed (and 44 percent fully agreed) with this statement: "I will not refer someone from my church to a purely secular mental health professional—I will only refer to a Christian professional." Only 29 percent were straightforwardly willing to refer to a non-Christian professional.

Yet even *with* Christian professionals, 72 percent of church leaders agreed or somewhat agreed (37 percent fully agreed) with this statement: "Even if I refer to a Christian professional, until I know I can trust that person, I still worry that they may give advice that is nonbiblical or damaging, or opposes the church's teaching." (For one in four—28 percent—that was not a concern.)

Adding to the complexity is that the provider needs to be a skilled counselor. One pastor on the survey captured the dilemma well, saying, "Bible-based counseling is important, but the counselor needs to be educated and trained to make it work well. Secular counseling training is also valuable. Sadly, most of the professionals in my area are atheist or agnostic, and their advice is frequently contrary to Scripture. This makes it extremely difficult to refer someone to them."

These concerns were among the reasons many pastors opt to develop a well-trained lay counseling ministry or band together with other churches to create a licensed counseling center—or both.

Combine Resources

One pastor we surveyed said, "Several local churches came together a few years ago to establish a Christian counseling center staffed with

Christian counselors from across the region. The services are open to the public too. This has provided great mental health services to the community and has branched out across a two-state area. We highly recommend this kind of model."

Trend #4: When pastors refer out, there's a tendency to lose touch.

One of the most striking findings on the entire survey was the response to a question about the wait time when they refer someone out.

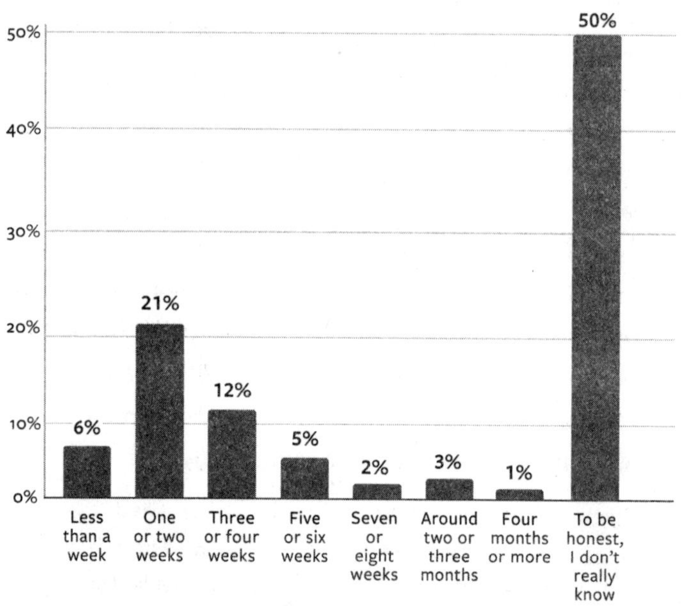

As you can see, by far the largest answer—exactly half of the pastors and church leaders—was "I don't really know." The implication is that upon making the referral, many pastors and ministry leaders don't necessarily know what happens next.

When we shared this survey result with a group of pastors in a focus group, they reacted with concern. They said they identified with not knowing this answer and said that with all the pressures pastors face and so many areas competing for their attention, it's not surprising many of them lose touch after delegating the need to someone else. Several of these pastors described this as an "aha" moment, recognizing that their referral system might be removing them too far from the care process.

All this said, the other half of the survey respondents did clearly have a way to know what happened. Many of them said they have a process in place to follow up with the person after they started counseling. As one pastor put it, "After a few meetings with someone, I can tell if we're making good progress or if they need something deeper. Often, it's both. Once I send them to a counselor, I'm not meeting with them as regularly and instead do check-ins. I ask, 'How is counseling going?' Now my role is to walk with them and be their cheerleader. My goal is to ensure that they have a biblical understanding of Christ and His love for them, and help them develop the spiritual disciplines they need."

Enlist a Volunteer Mental Health Coordinator

A common strategy for churches that couldn't afford a paid coordinator (to oversee lay helpers and stay in touch with referred-out counselees) was to enlist a practicing or retired medical or mental health professional for a few hours a week.

Trend #5: Referral options are often overwhelmed or simply unavailable.

As noted in the first chapter, one reason for the mental health crisis is that the supply of providers hasn't kept pace with the demand. As of 2024, more than one-third of the population of the United States lives in an area that the government designated as having a shortage of mental health care workers.[4]

The more specialized the practitioner, the more likely it is that they have long wait times or aren't taking new clients at all. For example, a 2023 study found that just 18.5 percent of psychiatrists were taking on new patients.[5] And the few who were had an average wait time of more than two months (sixty-seven days).

This shortage impacts the church. Seeking a Christian counselor is effectively a call for specialized care. As one pastor put it in a rather heart-wrenching comment on the survey, "We lack professional Christian counselors in our area. We have no one."

Because there is such high demand, Christian counselors tend to work long hours and have full caseloads, making it difficult for them to fit in new people quickly, or at all. One church counseling center director with several full-time therapists on staff explained, "Our dilemma is that we are so busy and have such demand that we are now having to see people every two to three weeks, which is not best practice, in my opinion—particularly at the beginning of therapy. If we feel like they need to meet weekly, we send them to a large outside network of counselors in private practice, specialists we have cultivated."

We asked him, "Do those counselors have room to see them?"

"Honestly . . . no. So that becomes a concern."

Even in areas where Christian counselors are available, finding the right fit can be a challenge. One leader shared about the acute need for individual counseling faced by a Black man in his fifties whose wife was planning to leave him. The only Christian counselors taking new clients were young white women in their twenties. Although licensed professionals are trained to serve anyone, it's understandable that the man was skeptical that these therapists would fully grasp his situation and concerns.

Create Virtual Options

If Christian counselors are rare in your area, many leaders recommended cultivating relationships with Christian counselors in other locations who will see your people virtually. Telehealth options often allow access to specialized providers as well. If appropriate, consider not only licensed professionals but also well-trained lay and biblical counselors and coaches. Review options through organizations listed in appendix 2 at Thechurchcares.com or ask pastors in other areas for recommendations.

Trend #6: Having a relationship with a mental health professional makes the difference for a quick response.

The main factor that improved wait times was whether the pastor had an official arrangement with a mental health professional—for example, a counseling center that agreed to hold several hours a week open for the members of that church. Just 19 percent of pastors had such an arrangement, but it appeared to be a highly effective strategy, exactly doubling the chances of getting someone an appointment quickly.

Among churches that have no special arrangements, just one-third (34 percent) of parishioners get in quickly (less than three weeks), with 37 percent having a wait time of five weeks or more. That pattern changes drastically when the pastor has even an *informal* relationship with a counselor who tries to accommodate their church. Sixty-two percent of those individuals are seen quickly, while just 13 percent must wait five or more weeks. Even better is when the church has an *official* arrangement with a professional: 70 percent of those individuals are seen quickly, with just 11 percent waiting five weeks or more.

Wait times for professional care depend on whether the church has a relationship with the professional.

Usual wait time to see a professional*	Church does not have an official arrangement (or does not apply/ not sure).	Church has no official arrangement, but certain professionals try to accommodate.	Church has an official arrangement with mental health professionals to get members in more quickly.	National average**
Less than a week	6%	16%	19%	13%
One to two weeks	28%	46%	52%	41%
Three to four weeks	29%	25%	19%	19%
Five or more weeks	37%	13%	11%	21%
*Excludes those who did not know. Percentages may not total 100% due to rounding.				
**Averages are likely improved from the true national average, as the source is pastors who were attuned to and following the referral.				

Offer Counselors Free Rent

A common model was offering counselors space rent-free, in exchange for reduced fees for church members. One external counseling center director said, "We have a dozen licensed professionals who see people at our center, and we realized that four or five of them had *time* to take on more clients, but all our space was maxed out. We partnered with churches so they could be on-site in their locations instead."

Trend #7: There will never be enough clinicians to meet the demand.

We frequently heard pastors say things to this effect: "The pandemic was brutal for mental health. I'll be glad when we get past this season and counselors aren't so booked up."

Unfortunately, the gap between mental health demand and supply is a long-standing structural problem that existed before the pandemic and won't be solved with our current mental health structure. This was the premise of my (Jim's) book *Beyond the Clinical Hour*, intended for clinicians and academics.

The National Center for Health Workforce Analysis reports that an additional 266,710 mental health professionals are needed to meet the current demand. They project that by 2036, that number will be 609,360.[6]

The good news is that if people want to go into the mental health field, they will never be out of work. The tragic news is that there's not a pathway to train more than a half million new therapists in the immediate future. And even if there were, there's not (and probably never will be) enough funding to pay the salaries of that many new clinicians.

This is why we're proposing that the church must help build a new culture and parallel system of care—one that relies on a wide scope of lay counselors, coaches, listeners, and other volunteers to meet the needs that are currently not being met.

Partner with a Service

Many pastors said they would like to have a clinician on-site but assumed it was impossible. Thankfully, multiple local and regional ministries place mental health professionals in churches and handle the paperwork and finances. The director of one such organization explained, "We always work with a pastor and ministry team at the church. We share space, create a mini counseling clinic, and handle everything that runs in the background—insurance, billing, electronic medical records, and so on. This is not us leasing space; we are developing a strong partnership with the church." Several examples of these services are provided in appendix 2. Or ask around to find these services in your area.

Trend #8: Most pastors agree that lay helping is important for mental health, but very few are doing it.

Here's something from the survey results that made us say *wow*: an astounding 94 percent of pastors and church leaders either fully or somewhat agreed with the statement "Most people with mental health issues can be greatly helped by spending time with a Christian lay counselor/coach who will listen to them and walk alongside them for a season." That's almost everybody!

Yet of those same leaders, only 38 percent were confident there were indeed laypeople in their church who had the basic training to help in that way, and only 33 percent had an official lay counselor or lay listener program such as Stephen Ministries or spiritual directors (rising to 38 percent when inner healing ministries were included).

That said, most churches (78 percent) said they *do* have lay-led, peer-group ministries that support and come alongside people in need in other ways. There are innumerable options—everything from weekly small groups and affinity-type groups (such as Bible studies, MomCo groups for moms with young children, or empty-nest fellowship groups) to targeted recovery programs, marriage ministries, or single-issue groups (such as GriefShare, DivorceCare, Pure Desire, or family advocacy ministries) to unique programs created by that local church or parish.

Can trained laypeople help? Do you have them?

	Disagree	Somewhat agree/ Somewhat disagree	Agree
Most people with mental health issues can be greatly helped by a Christian lay counselor/coach who will listen and walk alongside them for a season.	6%	32%	61%
Among those who agreed/somewhat agreed:			
We have laypeople who are adequately trained to address basic mental health needs.	38%	25%	38%
Note: Question wording shortened. Percentages do not total 100% due to rounding.			

Trend #9: Nearly all pastors agree that peer support is vital for fostering good mental health, although many hadn't thought about it that way before.

One intriguing and encouraging finding is that the large majority of pastors (86 percent) agree with this statement: "A community of believers supporting one another is one of the best ways to foster good mental health inside the church," with the ratio rising to 96 percent when including those who somewhat agree.

Having a supportive community not only helps address mental health distress but can also help *prevent* it. For decades, nearly every study looking at factors that improve mental health has concluded that building community and supportive, encouraging friendships is the secret sauce to maintaining and building great mental health.

In other words, peer-support ministry efforts—which most churches already have or can build—are often just as important for mental health as any other program. In our interviews, it was clear that pastors and other church leaders simply might not have thought about those ministries as a key piece of the mental health puzzle within their church.

The fact that these ministries already exist inside many churches should make it easier to adjust people's perception of them and to officially include them as part of a church's holistic mental health effort. Not only that, but hundreds of national and regional ministries (such as Stephen Ministries, The Church Cares, the American Association of Christian Counselors, the International Association of Catholic Mental Health Ministers, and many others) exist to help churches build these programs and train the trainers, who will then run the efforts within the church.

Trend #10: Pastors who already have an effective mental health ministry are more likely to see it as vital for discipleship and evangelism.

The vast majority of church leaders (96 percent) see mental health efforts as being either primarily for church members or equally for church members and for outreach. But the averages obscure an important truth we noted throughout our interviews. Churches that have a working, effective process are more likely to see mental health ministry efforts as an essential tool for discipleship and evangelism. For example, 74 percent of such churches saw it as at least partially for outreach, while churches without an effective process were more likely to see this area of ministry as only for church members (just 59 percent saw it as at least partially for outreach).

Do you see your mental health efforts as being more for church members, more as an outreach to the community, or equally both?

	Primarily outreach	More as outreach/ partially for church members	Equally for outreach and church members	More for church members/ partially outreach	Primarily for church members
National average	1%	4%	31%	32%	33%
Those with an effective mental health process	1%	4%	36%	33%	26%
Those without an effective mental health process	1%	5%	26%	27%	41%

Outreach efforts are also more likely to draw in reluctant church attenders. One pastor who had recently started a small counseling center at his church said, "One thing we learned is that a lot of people don't want to go to a sterile, unfamiliar place to talk to a stranger. So having this ministry on location at the church helps. And those who are not as familiar with the church see it as the place where they experience peace, hope, and safety. We have already found it's a good segue for them to feel like they can come here and be welcomed."

In addition, many pastors mentioned that having a ministry like this is the new wave of discipleship—enlisting and equipping church members to do the work of caring for one another well.

Yet there were quite a few pastors who held a different view. Whether leaders saw mental health ministry as part of discipleship and outreach appeared related to whether they viewed psychological issues as integrated with or distinct from emotional, relational, and spiritual concerns. When asked about his advice for those starting a mental health ministry, one pastor on the survey said, "Don't. As a church, you can support the person on their spiritual journey, discipleship, fellowship, and creating relationships with others. But their mental health requires other trained professionals, and it's good to keep it separate." Another pastor said, "Be willing to refer so as to not distract from the primary mission of making disciples."

As noted, however, many other church leaders—especially those with an effective, working mental health ministry—see this arena as explicitly about making disciples:

- "Mental health ministry has been vital to the discipleship of our church."
- "This is evangelism. This is what we are called to do as Christians."
- "Learning to be mental health lay ministers strengthens the faith and skills of church members."
- "A mental health ministry is really just an extension of your efforts to bring effective pastoral care to your faith

community. Don't be afraid to work with the people the Holy Spirit sends you!"

- "I believe mental health is one of the biggest mission fields for the church, and churches need to put as much effort into mental health efforts as other ministries of the church."

A church that has embraced this arena of ministry is Watermark Community Church, a congregation with ten thousand members in the Dallas–Fort Worth area. A significant portion of its discipleship program is organized around a recovery-ministry model known as re:generation, a model that is now used at many other churches. The director of the program, Nathan Graybill, shared a crucial perspective for other pastors considering some form of mental health ministry:

> We started with a different recovery-ministry model here, and it was actually a survey that changed our mind about what we needed to do. We surveyed all our participants and found that there were great things happening—people were experiencing authentic community, recovering from addictions, being healed of many things, being fully known and fully loved. But by various spiritual formation measures, they weren't necessarily growing in their knowledge and use of Scripture, understanding their identity in Christ, understanding and deploying their spiritual gifts, knowing how to share the gospel.
>
> Our mission isn't only to make sober Christians but to make fully devoted followers of Christ. So we decided to turn this whole area of ministry into a primary means of

discipleship for the church. These ministries are the one place where everybody shows up broken or hurting, and they're motivated to work. That doesn't happen in every environment of the church, so these are prime opportunities for discipleship. When we started infusing spiritual formation practices into the ministry and opened it up to the church, it grew and expanded. It's now in hundreds of churches around the country and internationally.

Ask Around

Many church leaders with a mental health ministry advised asking around as you get started with your own. One said, "This is an essential ministry to support believers and nonbelievers. Start small; reach out to faith-based programs and other churches who offer mental health ministries. Become educated!"

"Do *Something*"

Regardless of what type of ministry a church wants to do, the consistent advice from the survey was to step out and do *something*—whatever is consistent with the life and needs of your church and community. As one respondent put it:

> The gospel has a holistic approach to salvation. And God has certainly given every community of believers gifting to do SOMETHING but not everything. Find your church community mandate.

4

Building a Caring Church Ministry

A Map to This New World

> A world where the future is unknown cannot be inconsistent with planned and purposive action.
>
> C. S. LEWIS, *Letters to Malcolm: Chiefly on Prayer*

Not long ago, on a business trip to the Dominican Republic, I (Shaunti) was intrigued by the number of Santo Domingo tourist sites related to Cristóbal Colón (Christopher Columbus). While his reputation is tainted by his treatment of indigenous people, it's undeniable that his voyages of exploration mark a turning point in history. Sometimes people assume that Columbus "discovered" the New World because he was haphazardly sailing west to find a route to Asia rather than sailing around Africa. This isn't quite true. While he didn't have a map of the world, he did have a map of the wind!

Decades before Columbus, Henry the Navigator believed that winds over the Atlantic blew in a giant clockwise rotation. It was as if his theory was "What goes around comes around." Columbus knew that if mariners sailed south from Spain to the Canary Islands, the winds would push ships west. He figured that if he kept going west, the crew could eventually sail north and be pushed east to return home. So Columbus followed in Henry the Navigator's nautical footsteps as he headed west until he intercepted the New World. His first map was based on the ideas of others.

The vision we're proposing in this book is like a new world. To get there, we follow the maps of others. The specifics for each church will be different, but the winds—the forces that move ships and change people—are the same. Some churches and leaders have been sailing these seas for years and have much wisdom to share, and others have only recently started exploring but have created innovations we all can learn from. Even if these explorations feel new to you, there's plenty of help available from those who have gone before. A meaningful amount of the map has already been filled in, and other explorers are adding to it every day.

In this chapter, we'll share a big map to help you build out the CARE strategy at all levels of your church triangle, especially the lay listening efforts that may not yet be part of your church's culture of care.

First, let's remind ourselves what this new world looks like. The church strategy for Coordinated Attention, Restoration, and Encouragement (CARE) can be represented by our triangle models, which show coordinating the right level of care with the right level of need—and the importance of adding laypeople as caregivers.

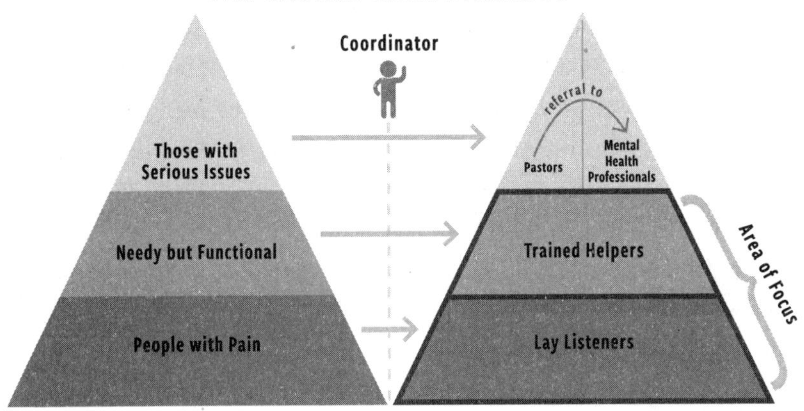

This chapter considers what the CARE strategy might look like in practice, covering four broad areas of focus: getting started, identifying the roles of key players, rolling out the strategy publicly, and connecting with The Church Cares initiative for training, engagement, and help, if desired. (Later chapters will zoom in on more detailed elements of the map, going beyond the *what* and into the *how*, focusing on what you as a leader need to know to make decisions. Part 2 of the book includes short overviews of the content that caregivers will learn, such as how to help someone manage their emotions, how to listen without trying to fix, and how to handle specific issues.)

We invite you to test the CARE strategy, put it into action, and adjust it to fit your church's culture. See if some version of this strategy works in your community and church, then help others in this space understand the winds and chart further paths for success.

Getting Started

As we walked through hundreds of conversations with church leaders, we sought input from those who could offer wisdom about building a mental health ministry involving all levels of the church triangle. We also spoke to multiple church leaders who were about to launch this sort of initiative and followed up with several of them six months to a year later.

Several common lessons emerged.

Lesson #1: Don't go it alone; tap the leaders who are called.

In our interviews with pastors and leaders, the first emerging message was to appoint a team. In nearly every situation, someone other than the pastor needs to be tasked to make a ministry like this happen. Pastors lead by appointing others to lead these initiatives.

The pastor is the captain of the ship that's exploring this new world, but they can't be the one trimming the sails, swabbing the deck, and cooking in the galley. The pastor must provide direction to those who are.

One pastor whose church has a vibrant mental health ministry advised this on the survey:

> We are called to shepherd the souls of our congregation. And we must not carry this alone. Carrying the burden alone can potentially lead to us, as the ministers, being in need of care as well. This begins with people in our church as a bridge to those outside the walls. I know it is uncomfortable at times, but we must do it.

Thus, the most crucial element of getting started with building a CARE strategy in your local church is to tap and bring in those who will lead the work under the guidance of the pastor.

Start with Who You Already Have

Multiple pastors suggested that for churches that don't have a professional clinician in the congregation, this ministry can get started without a clinical adviser on board at the beginning. They advised taking stock of the people already available to you rather than adding stress by trying to find people you think you "should" use. On the survey, one pastor recommended, "See who God has already placed in your midst in this area and start there."

Lesson #2: Some sort of working group is essential.

One of the first needs is a working group that can create and implement strategies as directed by the pastor and/or other leaders. This group will meet regularly to define needs, gather resources, give direction, provide options, advise the pastor, and implement approved proposals.

Note that at this phase, these volunteers are *not* providing care. They are helping set up the care strategy. Some of these people may indeed transition to the care phase, but the working-group phase requires a different skill set.

Many pastors launched such a team with an appeal from the pulpit for experienced people who might be interested in giving their time in this way. Other pastors privately went to a few trusted people to ask if they would jump in. The key is to identify people who have a calling to this kind of ministry. Based on the stories we heard, the

Holy Spirit has a way of tapping people on the shoulder and making it clear that they are to be part of this process.

Enlist a Mentor Church

Many pastors and working group facilitators said it was most helpful to find a mentor church that was a year or two ahead in the process, whose ministry organizer was willing to occasionally share advice over lunch or a video call. One pastor recommended, "Consult with another church that is currently doing this effectively."

Lesson #3: The working group needs a leader and diverse members.

It's common for one leader to run the working group, be the liaison to the pastor, and help select those with needed skill sets to be the other members.

Most churches had one or more mental health professionals on the team. Beyond that, we heard of successful working groups that included everyone from stay-at-home moms who were great at organization, to married couples who had gone through a marriage crisis and were now passionate about this type of ministry, to retirees with extra available time, to businesspeople with a heart for mental health and a handy connection to donors in the community. Having a team with diverse opinions and backgrounds helped ensure that broader needs were met and helped the team avoid getting stuck in groupthink.

Reallocate Specialized Volunteers

One mental health professional said, "I originally volunteered three or four hours a week in the children's ministry. But when this opportunity arose, we realized it was more important for me to take my time and skill set and use it to ensure that we have well-trained volunteers and help guide the pastor regarding mental health issues."

Lesson #4: Before a full rollout, try a pilot phase.

For any strategy that includes care by laity (not just the pastor or a professional), the most common next step is to recruit a few initial lay volunteers and conduct training. After that, the goal is to launch the strategy in a pilot phase before a full rollout.

We recommend recruiting one or more CARE coordinators. This might be the same person who is running the working group, or it could be someone else. Once the church provides care, the coordinator must be able to evaluate needs as they arise and determine what level of care is needed.

This new lay care ministry could be as robust as a comprehensive, highly trained lay counseling program (the "trained helper" level of the triangle) or as simple as a few basically trained lay listeners (the bottom level of the triangle) . . . or both.

The lay listening level of the triangle is both the low-hanging fruit and, according to our survey, what is most often missing from churches. That's why the primary focus of The Church Cares is to help churches build out that basic level of care.

Identifying the Roles of the Key Players

There are three roles that every church should consider when launching a mental health ministry that includes laypeople: the pastor, the coordinator, and the helper/caregiver.[1] You can read specifics about how these roles work in part 2, but here's a brief overview.

A Pastor Who Models Vulnerability and Casts a Vision of Care

A ship's captain doesn't stand watch for inclement weather, a fire chief doesn't put out fires, and a police chief doesn't catch criminals. Instead, these leaders oversee, inspire, and resource the team. To address the mental health crisis effectively, a pastor—especially the senior pastor—needs to launch, direct, and empower their team. Their job is to be involved without being the one who runs everything.

One senior pastor on the survey offered his top advice to those considering this kind of ministry: "Trust your leaders/lay leaders who have training and experience in this. Empower, support, and release them."

Leading the church in this area of mental health also requires a unique stance: vulnerability. Being open and transparent about living in the same broken world as everyone else, with the same needs, is the most powerful—and perhaps the most challenging—thing a church leader can do to transform the culture of the church.

A Coordinator Who Creates and Conducts the Strategy

As the ideas in this book were forming, I (Jim) was speaking to a group of about four hundred clinicians, presenting the need for the church to step into the gap of care around mental health. The attendees were about to be introduced to a new identity: not clinician, not counselor, but coordinator.

Seated at round tables with their peers, they described their lives as clinicians to the group. They introduced themselves by saying things like "I work in a [small, midsize, or large] private practice." "I see about [five, ten, twenty, or thirty] clients a week." "We are distinctly Christian in that we . . ."

With tens of millions of people not receiving the mental health care they need,[2] I asked them to think about what their practice would look like if, working out of the same office space, and with the same staff, they were responsible to care for ten thousand people each year instead of a few hundred. "If the responsibility to address the mental health needs of those in your community rested with *you*, what would you do?"

Looks of shock appeared on every face as they came to grips with the scale of need that existed outside their office doors. Then the room buzzed with conversation about how they would meet this task.

The broad consensus was that they would have to change their focus from being *the* provider of service to being the overseer of services that included different levels of care. One professional said bluntly, "One person can't do all that—I would have to get a lot of help."

That conversation helped form the basis for the coordinator role.

Coordinators play a central role in implementing the CARE strategy. Let's revisit our triangle graphic.

THE CHURCH CARE STRATEGY

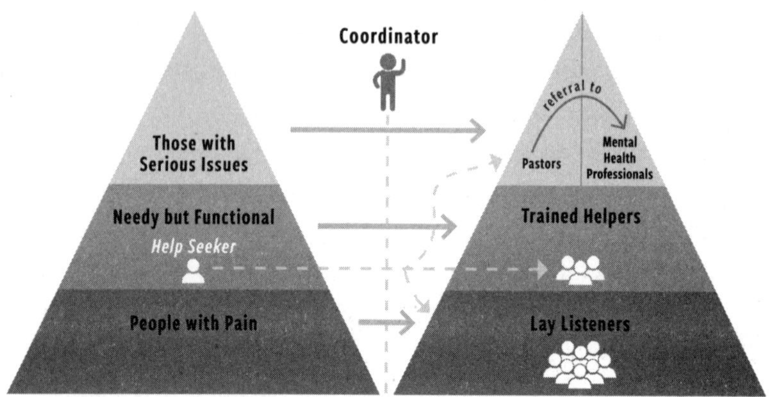

The coordinator may be paid or a volunteer, a contractor or a staff member. Either way, they hold one or both of two key roles. (These will be unpacked further in part 2.)

1. The coordinator is a decision-maker. This is the central person who conducts the intake with someone who is seeking help; they understand the need and ensure that the help seeker gets funneled to the right type of care at all levels of the triangle. The coordinator also supervises the lay caregivers.
2. The coordinator may also be the person running the ministry, taking the vision of the pastor, the church leadership, and the working group (which they may have been part of) and transforming those ideas into action.

Sometimes those roles are held by different people because they require different skill sets. For the sake of simplicity, in this book we assume that the same person holds both roles.

So who should be the coordinator? This person is often a clinician, well-trained coach, or a care pastor or staff member with some sort of relevant training. The large church with a robust lay counseling program that we described in chapter 2 had a licensed clinical social worker who funneled people to the right care and ran the ministry.

But we also have seen many coordinators who are not clinicians. For example, Lynn is on the staff of a large church and serves as a ministry director. She has a seminary degree, and while she has never practiced as a mental health professional, she has some training in human care and is highly regarded by various clinicians. She attributes her success as a coordinator to being an organizer of people and to understanding their heart needs. She acknowledges the limitations of not being a clinician but makes up for that by seeking guidance and involvement from therapists in the church and the community, especially when unique or challenging issues arise.

Above all, the right coordinator grasps the idea of being responsible for the ten thousand. Rather than being the lone pastoral counselor, coordinators reproduce themselves as the care matcher, trainer, overseer, and supporter of the team.

What Lay Listeners Can Do

The Church Cares has identified key tasks that are appropriate for lay listeners and created routes for training. The topics of these short online training modules permit a glimpse of the purpose and function of some caregivers, including:

- How to pray with those in distress
- Listening and the ministry of presence
- Dealing with emergencies

- What the Bible says about pain
- How grief can be good
- How to help families in distress
- Talking to adolescents
- Habits and addictions
- Being an encourager
- Sitting with intense emotions (sadness, anger, and fear)
- Helping those who have known trauma

A Caregiver Who Will Serve, Support, Strengthen, and Inspire

The third focus is the person who is actually offering care. In part 2, we dive into this role in more detail so pastors know what training tasks are needed to prepare lay helpers. The key is that these individuals ultimately care for the person in need through listening and the ministry of presence.

Caregivers can be found in every church; there are often many people interested in this ministry. They may go through basic lay listening training, or they may receive more involved instruction so they can provide lay counseling or coaching at the trained helper level.

Paul describes one of the qualities of an elder (or overseer) as being "gentle" or "patient" (1 Timothy 3:3, NIV). That's the image of a caregiver: someone who has patience, is not overly reactive, and offers a calming presence. On the survey, one pastor offered this as her top advice to lay helpers: "Your response to someone, when they open up to you about their struggle, is key in helping them know that it is good to ask for help."

Lay caregivers can't and don't fix things. (Good licensed professionals can't fix things, either, and they don't try; their job is to empower and equip the person to address those things themselves.) There is a beautiful theology underneath the "we can't fix things for you" concept. It is the Holy Spirit who moves in the hearts of people, heals the infirm, makes straight the paths to justice, and corrects evil. As Paul writes, "We have this treasure in jars of clay to show that this all-surpassing power is from God and not from us" (2 Corinthians 4:7, NIV).

This passage challenges us to be the clay pots that contain and offer God's power and authority. Paul also suggests that we know pain, suffering, and hardship so that we might reveal life. A good caregiver can promote life growth in others by letting the Holy Spirit work through the pain, being a comforter on the journey, and helping the person draw closer to Christ. That's one reason most churches involved in mental health ministry see it as a key part of the discipleship mission of their church.

The greatest challenge for new caregivers—and the greatest relief for seasoned helpers—is the realization that we are not responsible for rescuing, fixing, delivering, and protecting everyone in their unique hardships. We are called to be present—to act as Christ's ambassadors and let God move in difficult situations. Caregivers are given a front-row seat to the beauty of God being present in tragedy, suffering, and restoration.

Create Community Among Caregivers

The weight of confidential care could lead to lay listeners feeling isolated and burdened. In addition to offering official supervision, consider creating community, cohesion, and encouragement among caregivers via a group text thread, occasional social opportunities, or a shared meal at supervision meetings.

Rolling Out the Strategy Publicly

Because congregational investment in a mental health ministry is so important, thinking through the rollout and the ministry's ongoing integration into the life of the church is just as important as creating the program itself. For this reason, many churches find it helpful to invest in five strategies when they launch a ministry of care.

Creating a Caring Culture in the Church

Most church members today are supportive of the *concept* of mental health ministry in the church—for those "other people" who have need. Leaders can consider how to prepare church members for not just caring but being cared for by others. *Seeking* help requires humility, as it challenges every voice in our heads that says, *Don't let them see you sweat,* even though we're all perspiring profusely. It isn't difficult for people who have already been broken by the weight of life, who have matured through the gauntlet of suffering, to seek support. Receiving care is refreshing for them. But receiving care is a challenge for those who see themselves as self-sufficient, independent, and put together. The latter description is our cultural norm.

This is why creating a culture of care is so critical. The ministry of care can reach its full potential when the culture of a church is characterized by people who see their own need for grace and ask for help, rather than by people who say, "I don't want to be a burden." Over time, we need to change the view that "Will you help me?" is a shameful request, and instead view it as a normal question that should be asked by everyone at different times.

A true care culture will help all those in the church recognize that just about everyone needs their back scratched, their hand held, or their shoulder hugged. Which means just about everybody needs to be taught to be effective back scratchers, hand holders, and shoulder huggers.

Make It Easy

As some people are uncomfortable with the idea of needing help and struggle to reach out to the church, one survey taker advised, "Make the next step super clear for people who need help. For example, we put the contact info of three counselors we recommend on signs in our restrooms and our auditorium."

Ongoing Communication

Ongoing vision casting and "we are here" communication with church members is essential—and it needs to start from the top. This communication may be arranged and planned by the coordinator, but the senior pastor will need to be one of the key voices casting the vision and ensuring that people know this is an important direction of the church.

One of the consistent pieces of advice from those who already have a mental health ministry was to ensure that the church leadership is vocal about their endorsement of the program:

- "The conversations that break the stigma and introduce mental health into the church are best received when they initially come from senior leadership."
- "Preach mental health from the pulpit. Normalize it. Encourage it. Support it. Explain it."

- "A church has to see its leadership invested in and championing a ministry in order to take it seriously."
- "This is absolutely vital, and it needs to start from the pulpit. Teach about it, destigmatize it, get help and support for yourself and your marriage, lead out of a place of health, and be open about needing/getting help and support yourself."

Having the mental health ministry as a visible, normalized part of the church goes a long way toward integrating it into the life of the congregation. One pastor on the survey said, "We share our building with a Christian counseling center. This has made a huge impact on the way people view mental health counseling, simply by having it constantly in their line of sight."

Use the Contact Card

Many churches have contact cards for visitors and attenders to share prayer needs, to indicate interest in joining a small group, or to update contact information. As a way to identify those who might benefit from the mental health ministry, leaders suggested adding a line that asks, "Would you like a call back from someone in our care ministry?"

Basic Training for All Leaders

Another helpful strategy is to offer training that goes beyond those directly involved in the mental health ministry. Many churches with successful ministries mentioned the need to train *all* leaders (and perhaps even all volunteers across the church) in basic aspects of listening—both so leaders have the basic skills and so they know how to funnel those in need to the CARE coordinator. Other churches and mental health professionals stressed the importance of any leader understanding how to spot when someone might be at risk for self-harm and how to get that person help.

One pastor we interviewed described how all leaders in the church receive basic lay listening training:

> This class is just a few hours, and it isn't under any type of psychological framework. It simply communicates that if someone comes to you and they're in distress, here's how you listen. Here's how you walk through helping that person ask themselves the right questions to navigate toward solutions. Here's how you integrate prayer and faith into the conversation with someone. Every one of our members has the opportunity to take that class. But we also require it of anybody who's a leader in our church. If you're going to head up a small group or run a team of volunteers, you can't be a leader without taking it.

Another pastor said that their primary lay listening volunteers (their spiritual facilitators) go through robust training that starts with reading a book on listening and continues with in-depth training over the course of several months. He also clarified, "We ask *every* volunteer in our church to read the same book on listening. If they're part of the parking ministry or if they're stacking chairs, we want them to at least know the basics. Anyone could encounter someone who needs to be referred to our spiritual facilitators."

Enlist Modern Biblical Counseling Resources

If a pastor desires a biblical counseling approach, there are multiple biblical counseling groups and schools that offer robust training and certification for volunteer laypeople and those making biblical counseling a vocation.[3]

Educational Events and/or Community Building

Multiple church leaders mentioned the importance of having the mental health ministry host educational events or seminars. This increases visibility for the initiative, conveys helpful content, and builds community for those involved. As one pastor pointed out, "Prevention classes are vital to help people *before* issues get to an emergency level."

Many pastors also enlisted specialists from the community to conduct educational seminars on common issues (such as anxiety, marriage, and trauma). They found that these events not only were a blessing for the congregation but were also a way to reach the broader geographic area and give people an introduction to the church. Several other church leaders mentioned that these broader events became the foundation for an entirely new type of community. After their church was impacted by a tragedy, one women's ministry director we spoke to became a champion for mental health ministry in her church—and others. She told us,

> We now regularly bring people together around mental health. And it's not a support group: it's a community. This

is a regular gathering for people who live with mental health challenges or have family members who do. Everybody who walks in the door has already identified as having a vested interest; nobody asks you why you're there. People sit at tables, there's fellowship, there's community around what we're going through, and it's a safe place to talk about these things. There's also a speaker so they can get accurate psychoeducation. For example, we recently had a speaker who shared about the trauma therapy EMDR.

There's great bonding from being with other people who have the same needs. This community is so important. For example, in various places there are retreats for moms who have children with serious mental illness. They get out of the car and burst into tears because with everybody there, they don't have to explain or defend themselves. They don't have to deal with the stares or the judgments. They don't even know each other, but they fall into each other's arms, weeping. I'm telling you, community is so important.

Offer Group Sign-Ups at Events

Church leaders suggest using events as a means to funnel uninvolved people to peer groups, where they can receive ongoing support. Announce sign-ups for specific groups (such as AA, women's Bible studies, job networking groups, or empty-nester groups), and have group leaders follow up the next day to welcome them.

Specific Care for Pastors and Staff

It was common during interviews to hear pastors say that somewhere along the way they realized a pathway for church staff care needed to be an essential part of their mental health ministry, especially since pastors and staff usually needed confidential, off-site care. Multiple churches, even some very small ones, said that allocating budget for pastors and staff members to get professional counseling was one of the best possible uses of their funds.

As one pastor advised on the survey, "The emotional health of your staff and small group leaders is more important than most other developmental strategies in the church."

We spoke with one leader who runs a ministry for church staff members. He said, "All our energy has gone to the top of the church in the last twenty to thirty years. The adage is 'As long as the top is healthy, the whole is healthy.' But I don't know if that's true. We've gone after that, but we haven't necessarily seen those results. What if we can make the *entire* church staff healthy? The more we get in the weeds with church staff, the more we realize we haven't shepherded the staff—and they are responsible for the entire congregation."

Mental Health Coverage on the Insurance Plan

One pastor of a midsize church said, "One thing we did when choosing our health care plan was to make sure mental health services were free. So our folks on staff never have to worry about that. It's treated the same way as seeing their primary doctor; they only pay a co-pay. They can go to therapy as many sessions as needed. We value that."

Connecting with The Church Cares

If you feel overwhelmed and wonder how on earth to implement all these suggestions, remember that a great deal of the map of this "new world" has already been filled in by those who have gone before.

The ministry initiative we have mentioned, The Church Cares, exists to help you. It provides resources and connects you to other mapmakers and explorers. The resources available through The Church Cares serve as a warehouse of information to take to your church—of any size, shape, or demographics—and provide the tools you need to succeed.

If you'd like to explore getting help, please sign up (or have your point person sign up) at Thechurchcares.com to find out how to implement the CARE strategy in your church. The resources provided there are our effort to share materials beyond what can be offered in a book and are continually being developed and updated. As this is a nonprofit ministry, the site includes a free clearinghouse for information, tools, and resources developed by our team and others worldwide (and shared with their permission). This includes instructional videos and manuals for pastors, coordinators, and caregivers, as well as templates that might be useful for intake, assessment, informed consent, legal matters, and more. The Church Cares team is continually assessing and offering new material produced by other ministries as well.

Being Part of the 24/7 Online Mental Health Support Trend

Becoming part of The Church Cares community also allows churches to be networked through 7 Cups, our partner technology platform, which was named for a Chinese poem about no longer feeling alone and troubled.

You might be picturing a start-up tech company with a website. It's not! A line from the movie *The Avengers* might serve as a good metaphor. Iron Man/Tony Stark is being blunt with the Avengers' nemesis, Loki, about what's about to happen.

> Tony Stark: When they come, and they *will*, they'll come for you.
>
> Loki: I have an army.
>
> Tony Stark: We have a Hulk.[4]

If a church wishes to build its church care ministry rapidly, effectively, simply, and to a community-changing scale to help all who come—and they *will* come—this platform allows you to say, "We have a Hulk!" As one of the world's largest chat-based peer support networks, 7 Cups is already used by millions of people in business and government in dozens of languages. After this platform was developed, it was realized that if a business, a university, or a government entity could use 7 Cups to enlist lay care for their people, so could the church.

The relationship between The Church Cares and 7 Cups allows care programs to be built to scale so that churches can collaborate and support one another, and do so in every country and in every language. Most importantly, using this app or online platform, your lay caregivers and those in need can connect organically, in a text thread, as they have time. This is an important addition for many who are looking for ongoing friendship and support, beyond a "once a week in the church office" conversation.

This partnership allows for some other useful elements if desired:

- Everyone in need can receive a response from The Church Cares–trained lay listeners around the world 24/7, even when your local church team is not available. This can be very valuable when someone is simply feeling alone late at night.
- Your church's team of lay listeners can provide Christian care to those in your local community (and beyond) if you would like that to be part of your ministry.
- Your church itself can be listed as part of the popular and searchable 7 Cups network, providing a great way to reach your community and bring new people into your church.
- Pastors, leaders, coordinators, and caregivers can be mentored, supported, and trained by other church ministries. The best ideas can be circulated and implemented.

It's important to mention that 7 Cups is, like most large social media platforms, not a uniquely Christian portal. Thankfully, those who come in through the church can access a specifically Christian part of the online community, with specific training, resources, and lay listeners. Churches can tailor what their people see. In the big picture, we are thrilled that churches now have an official place on the platform, just as so many secular organizations do—which provides the opportunity to connect with people who might not hear a Christian perspective otherwise.

Any church can learn about and use the 7 Cups resource through The Church Cares website.

Trust God to Guide Your Process

As one pastor said on the survey, "Don't put it off. Get a group of people trained in mental health first aid and accompaniment, and trust the Lord to guide you each step of the way. Start small and grow from there."

Add to the Map

The marker of success for effective church caring ministry is a culture, not a program. We've seen hundreds of churches develop a culture that truly beckons to those in need and cares for them well, including many programs that started small.

One pastor offered her top advice:

> Mental health ministry isn't optional anymore. You need a plan that works, given the gifts and limitations of your church. You don't have to do everything, but you can do something, even if it is a referral and then offering community and walking with the person while they seek help, without shame or stigma.

As you move forward, we hope you'll share what you learn with others and add to the map. Ultimately, we're mapping not a series of to-dos but a vision for a new world, where people in pain can receive care in the name of the One who came to bind up the brokenhearted.

One pastor put it this way: "Trust that it's not your ministry but, in fact, the Lord's. He may be calling you to love people where they are so He can meet them there."

5

"But What About . . . ?"

Answers to Common Concerns

Nothing in life is to be feared, it is only to be understood.
Now is the time to understand more, so that we may fear less.

MARIE CURIE

An amusing comment by billionaire investor Warren Buffett cautions against the type of person who says, "Well, it may be all right in practice, but it will never work in theory."[1] A big concern like the mental health crisis requires creative, bold solutions.

But it's one thing to suggest bold solutions. The real question remains: "Will it work?"

This chapter addresses those concerns and shares how these kinds of ministries are working in churches around the country. We respond to nine questions frequently raised by pastors in our research. There is no one right answer to these questions, as every church is unique and the Lord will almost certainly guide each one along a different path. We simply encourage every reader to, as Henry Blackaby so memorably put it, watch for where the Lord is working and join Him there.[2]

How can we launch a mental health ministry when we are already so busy with other priorities?

As noted earlier, while most pastors are involved in counseling at some level (on the survey, fully 75 percent said their churches offered counseling by the pastoral team), most also see referrals as the default beyond a certain number of visits or a certain point of complexity. Usually, even if the pastor wants to do more counseling and feels capable of it, they usually don't have the time. Eighty percent said they fully or somewhat agreed with this statement: "The current mental health need in my church is greater than I can address alone."

Many pastors see referrals to a counseling center in the same way that building maintenance might be outsourced to a facilities firm. Mental health needs can seem so diverse, complicated, and time-consuming that it feels easier to let the "experts" handle it. At the same time, many also view care ministry as a central task of the church. A pastor referring help seekers to clinicians can feel like they're jettisoning part of the church's purpose and sending people away from the church. But what else can they do?

Thankfully, there's a way through this dilemma. In one focus group, church staff and lay leaders who had already built a mental health ministry were asked what advice they would give another pastor considering a similar program. This is how the women's ministry director responded:

> Look, if I'm a church pastor and someone tells me, "You need to set up this ministry," I'm going straight into

> A-fib. I'm maxed! No matter how essential it is, the pastor absolutely cannot think of it that way. Instead, I would ask the pastor to consider this question: "Do you have people in your flock whose hearts beat for this?" Take three minutes onstage, present the need, and see if someone good comes to you. Let *them* investigate what other churches are doing and potentially find a reproducible framework. See what God sets up. Every church needs this, but your role as pastor isn't to do it. Your role is to see if God brings you a wingman who can.

One pastor reflected on his original objections to creating a mental health ministry. He said, "I hate to say it, but for most of us, the question is all about 'How will this ministry make my life easier as a pastor? What's in it for me? With everything else going on, how can I justify putting time into this?' And for me the answer was all about a pinch of prevention versus a pound of cure. A ministry like this is far better for your people, and it takes a huge load off you."

Other pastors agreed. On the survey, one shared his top advice to churches considering a mental health ministry: "This will save you time and energy as a pastor as well as provide better care for those who need mental health care."

And we can't get around the fact that care is needed. As another pastor on the survey pointed out, having some sort of in-house ministry is "unavoidable now. . . . The shepherd knows the condition of their flock. People are hurting, and we need to be prepared and equipped to help them."

What if our church is too small to host this type of ministry?

Many small churches worry that they don't have the people, space, or finances to create a CARE ministry from scratch. Thankfully, there are many ways to accomplish the same type of goal. Here are three.

First, one of the goals of The Church Cares is to help such churches. Connecting with a facilitator ministry like ours gives church leaders access to resources and help from others, such as free training materials.

Second, small churches may opt for a joint venture with other churches. One church leader offered this advice:

> If you are a small church, link arms with other churches who are committed to this effort. Create a joint venture. Maybe it's just with laypeople, or maybe it's with providers in the community. Maybe you decide on one centralized location where everyone from those churches can go to see someone, or maybe it's a rolling clinic that meets at a different church one day a week.

It doesn't take long to get a helpful scale. For example, if you have ten small churches, just one person from each congregation might end up being trained as a lay counselor. Now you have ten lay counselors. You can rotate people to different congregations or parishes when volunteers need a break or when a person seeking care would prefer to see someone who isn't part of their church.

Third, much of the CARE strategy involves affirmatively thinking through how to use what's already happening as a method of care.

Small steps like connecting people to small groups, providing space for a local recovery ministry, or having regular church dinners where people can fellowship over a meal may seem simple, but for someone who is isolated and in need, it can be life-changing.

Isn't engaging in mental health care risky without extensive training?

On our survey, more than two-thirds (68 percent) of pastors agreed or somewhat agreed (38 percent fully agreed) with this statement: "One main reason I refer to a professional is because I worry that I won't know what to say or do, or I worry about causing harm." Nine in ten (89 percent) agreed or somewhat agreed (54 percent fully agreed) that "helping someone with mental health issues is risky without extensive training."

One family pastor had a telling reaction when asked what his church's process would be if someone came forward for prayer with a mental health need. He said, "Well, if it's a young person, we would refer them to the youth pastor, or if it's a marriage issue, I would talk to them, and so on."

I asked, "Okay, but what if it's actually anxiety, or depression, or someone wrestling with PTSD from a sexual assault?"

He leaned away with a very uncomfortable look on his face. "I'll be honest. I feel like you just told me, 'Hey, Paul, that guy at the altar needs triple bypass surgery. Here's a scalpel.' Like, I know where the heart is and how blood works, but I would be so scared to take that first cut, because I'm not trained. That's how I feel about mental illness. It just seems so complex."

That reaction encapsulates the deep and often unspoken fear of many pastors: *What if I mess someone up?* And that's a legitimate concern; we have all heard stories about inept caregivers who *have* said or done damaging things. Although we believe those cases are the exception and get a disproportionate amount of attention today, it's still true that this type of ministry must be conducted with oversight and commitment to ethical standards. Yet as one therapist ruefully put it, "You think a licensed counselor can't mess someone up?"

Pastor, author, clinical psychologist, and mental health researcher Siang-Yang Tan of Fuller Seminary has been studying such concerns for years. In our interview, he smiled a bit sadly when we asked about nonprofessionals doing harm, and said:

> About 10 percent of psychotherapy is harmful too. Pastors can do damage, but so can professionals. Remember, psychology is a Johnny- or Jane-come-lately. Soul care has been going on for thousands of years before psychology came on the scene. The research shows that lay counselors can be helpful and effective with relatively minimal training, although professionals are often not aware of that.
>
> The Bible teaches us to reach out to one another, love one another, and bear one another's burdens. You don't stop helping people just because there's potential for harm. A small group leader or any ministry leader can potentially do harm. There is always a possibility for that, so you just learn how to do the best you can. Pastors shouldn't feel threatened

by the task before them, but pray for protection as they serve the Lord and minister to people.

As a church leader, you will need to address with sobriety the potential risks associated with care ministries, just as you do with children's ministry or security or building maintenance. The weight of responsibility doesn't mean you shouldn't do this ministry; it merely suggests that you shouldn't do it dumb (in Jim's words).

The church must follow our calling to care for others. We make it a point to be present in the peak and valley moments of life—at birth, at death, at weddings, at hospitals, and at graduations. What therapists can't do, churches do in abundance.

An effective care ministry is simply the church being empowered to sit with people in pain. This ministry is not new but has existed for two thousand years. To the degree that some aspects of that ministry have been minimized or lost over the years, there is great abundance in reclaiming it.

Skeptical? Attend a Lay Counseling Supervision Meeting.

If a pastor is concerned about the quality of lay counseling, one option is to find a friendly church that will allow the pastor to sit in on a supervision meeting or a training session. One lay counseling leader said, "If a pastor is on the outside looking in, I would invite them to one of our supervision sessions. We've had pastors from other churches come here because they started out concerned and wanted to investigate. Most of them ended up implementing a similar program at their church. We even trained a few of their people in our academy."

Can minimally trained laypeople actually be effective?

The simplest answer is yes. According to much research, both the "trained helper" and the "lay listener" levels of care can be very effective, given the right training and practice, and given they stay in their lane of care.[3] No one challenges the overwhelming evidence of effective lay-led church programs with passionately committed Christ followers who, with basic training, are addressing needs for people dealing with pornography, body image, blended families, addiction, single parenting, grief, divorce, and many other issues. The church is doing it here, there, and wherever there's need. What we are seeking is comprehensive organization and training to help the church become capable of greater impact.

It's important to note that adding those two levels of care is a solution that's not unique to the American church. Across the globe, developing countries have wrestled with the same need, simply because there might be only a few dozen highly trained mental health specialists in the region or, in some cases, the whole nation.

Siang-Yang Tan also pointed out:

> In the professional sphere, more and more people all over the world are researching lay caregiving. In the US, and around the world, psychologists are saying we need to use lay counselors more since we don't have enough professionals. In cases where mental health professionals are warning pastors and volunteers against doing lay care, it's likely because they aren't aware of the latest literature.
>
> In the US, we often have the option of professional referrals when needed. But also, remember that referrals

aren't just for sending people to professionals. Sometimes they're to a small group or to a couple doing marriage mentoring. I speak as a professional when I say that professionals aren't everything.

For example, consider the creative Friendship Bench idea from Zimbabwe (see sidebar). If it works in Zimbabwe, why shouldn't we have brigades of minimally trained grandmothers or grandfathers at thousands of local churches in the US?

The Friendship Bench[4]

In 2007, Dr. Dixon Chibanda was one of only twelve psychiatrists in Zimbabwe. Although the nation had little financing or facilities for mental health care, it did have one abundant resource: grandmothers. Dr. Chibanda created the Friendship Bench program and trained grandmothers, who were often already well-known volunteers in each community, in "strong listening skills, an ability to convey empathy and an ability to reflect."[5] He supported them via a digital scheduling tool on their phones. Local medical facilities conducted screenings of those in need. If someone was found to be sad and discouraged, but not so overwhelmed and depressed that they required medical intervention, they were referred to the Friendship Bench program. Conversations with the assigned grandmother took place at a literal wooden bench in each community—six sessions of listening and problem-solving therapy for those who needed care. The grandmothers also had regular meetings with one another to reflect on their sessions, provide advice, and decide on various directions.

Dr. Chibanda conducted a clinical trial of the program and found that lay helpers talking through life challenges with someone for about thirty minutes a week for about six weeks produced significant improvements in the person's feelings of sadness and discouragement. He summarized in a WHO report: "We found that after nine months the Friendship Bench patients had a significantly lower risk of symptoms than the standard of care group."[6]

Wouldn't it be safer to stick with trained professionals?

Although pastors and other church leaders may see the benefit of a lay caregiver strategy, they may also wonder if it's just safer to stick with trained professionals. That's a legitimate question. But our interview and survey participants often stressed something that's easy to forget: with costs so high and demand for mental health services far outpacing supply, a leader's choice is not usually between skilled and less skilled care but between some form of care and no care at all.

One church-based lay counselor put it this way:

> A big part of any lay counseling or lay coaching program is knowing our scope of practice. There's a certain amount I'm trained to handle, and I know the limits of my scope. Yes, with any caregiver, there is potential for harm. But there's equal potential for harm if this person remains alone. If I'm with this person, at least I have the potential to do some good. But if I'm too scared of doing harm and therefore don't do anything, the opportunity for help is lost. I need to know when the situation is getting beyond my limits and when to call for help myself. But within the limits and bounds, without our lay counseling program, who else would this person have?

A pastor and denominational leader was emphatic about the role of lay programs: "If I give someone a safe place within the church, I've created something that they've been looking for. If they come to the church for help and the church doesn't have it, what are they going to do? They'll go to somebody else or something else to find comfort. And odds are, that something else *will* do damage."

On our survey, it was revealing that licensed and highly trained professionals were less concerned than pastors about having someone provide mental health care without extensive training. While 55 percent of pastors fully believed it was risky, 44 percent of licensed professionals did.

This difference might be because clinicians are aware of research on lay counselor effectiveness. In the 1960s, researchers Robert Carkhuff and Charles Truax found that lay counselors were as effective as professional counselors in many (although not all) contexts.[7] Hundreds of studies since then have affirmed the effectiveness of lay care when unlicensed helpers are supported, supervised, and trained.

Both on the survey and in our interviews, mental health professionals emphasized that the real level of risk generally depends on the complexity of the situation and whether the nonprofessional understands when to enlist someone with more training.

How do lay caregivers know when they can help and when they might cause harm?

Ideally, the coordinator should make this decision for them. As mentioned in chapter 4, this is one of the main reasons to have a coordinator; they can conduct some form of intake and prevent a lay caregiver from stepping into a situation they're not prepared for in the first place.

Even with an effective coordinator, it's important for the caregiver to have the needed training about their role. This doesn't mean they're trained to be a "quasi clinician"; they're trained to be a *non*-clinician. They receive training so they can provide appropriate relational care as a Christ follower who extends the compassion of Jesus. As the apostle Paul put it, "The fruit of the Spirit is love, joy, peace, longsuffering, gentleness, goodness, faith, meekness, temperance: against such there is no law" (Galatians 5:22-23, KJV).

In other words, there are no "licensing restrictions" on doing good! Caregivers are not fake clinicians; they are people who offer the presence of joy, peace, patience, goodness, and so on. These are healing qualities, and when people are in pain, it's easy to lose them. A Christ-following lay caregiver can help restore them.

It's essential for *all* types of caregivers to recognize situations that are outside their responsibility. A licensed clinician can offer therapy and interventions, but professional boundaries restrict them from caring for clients outside specific and defined limits. (For example, a professional can't go to a barbecue at a client's house as a friend.) Lay caregivers are the other way around. They can't offer clinical interventions; they offer companionship. Both promote healing.

Even without training, most of us have walked with someone through grief, confusion, heartbreak, and pain. God has given us all important tools, such as compassion, empathy, a listening ear, and the simple power of presence. But with some basic training and oversight, lay caregivers will know how to do that better and receive two additional tools: knowledge about what they can and can't do, and discernment to help them know whether a situation is in the clinical area and needs to be addressed by someone trained to meet the clinical need.

One associate pastor we spoke with described how his church had developed a robust CARE-type framework.

> When I first learned about this program, it was described to me this way: we are putting laypeople on the front lines and telling them, "If you are out of your depth, escalate it." There are clear lines—everyone has a leader they can escalate to, and the leader can escalate it too.
>
> That system completely changed my perspective. It's so cool that laypeople know they are supported and they don't have to be afraid of stepping in to help. Because they know that if they find themselves in over their head, they have people who can support them.

Is it realistic to create a full-service center with licensed professionals, even if we wanted to?

The CARE model includes planning for all levels of care, including licensed clinicians who can be trusted to provide guidance consistent with biblical truth and church teaching. Many church leaders expressed a desire for a counseling clinic with licensed professionals on-site so they could have some oversight and coordination with these professionals.

Some churches we talked to had already gone through the process of creating such a clinic. (For more on how ongoing oversight and coordination can happen, see chapter 6.) Yet most church leaders felt something of this scope was out of reach.

But is it?

The decision about whether to tackle something that involves licensed clinicians will be highly individual. It will probably be influenced by the rules in your state and whether you have the capacity to jump all the hurdles. But if you feel called to have a full-service counseling clinic, don't assume it isn't an option.

Not long ago, on a sunny Sunday morning, I (Shaunti) was about to speak at a midsize church with my husband, Jeff. The senior pastor was showing us around a brand-new extension of their lobby. The walls had been painted the day before, and a host of scattered couches and tables were still shrink-wrapped. A portion of the new lobby would be allocated for a coffee shop, and an attractive divider led into a suite of comfortable rooms.

"That's our new counseling center," he said. "We're launching a sort of tiered system: one-on-one mentoring, lay counseling and coaching, peer groups, and licensed professionals."

I swiveled around. "Really?" This pastor had no idea I was in the middle of cowriting this book. His next words brought me up short.

"Yeah," he said with a chuckle. "One year ago, when we realized we needed *something*, we thought we were just starting with the basics. I thought maybe a bit of space would allow life coaches to meet clients here or give marriage mentors a place to connect with a couple. I had no idea we were signing up to be a full-on HIPAA-compliant facility! But the moment we began exploring the idea of including licensed professionals, it was as if God blew every door open. It was a lot of work, but it couldn't have been more clear that this is what we were supposed to do."

What if the church gets sued?

We went into this research expecting most pastors to be attuned to concerns about litigation and liability. But while those concerns exist (and we address specific solutions in chapter 6 and appendix 1), they were less common than anticipated.

On the survey, two out of ten church leaders (21 percent) agreed with this statement: "I am concerned with the liability of church-based mental health care ministries and that the church could be sued." That number rose to 51 percent when including those who somewhat agreed. One ministry director explained why his church decided to have no lay caregivers and use only professionals: "We are a litigious society. It's well and good to want to do good in the name of Jesus, but you've got to be as wise as a serpent and as gentle as a dove. We are constantly looking at this ministry with a certain amount of anxiety. That anxiety sometimes creates a quick no when maybe there could be a finessed yes."

However, many churches had come to terms with potential liability issues. One pastor pointed out, "You can be sued because a life group leader says the wrong thing too. I think most church pastors have accepted that risk, or they wouldn't be running a church. These days, most churches have liability policies that cover such issues. Only a small number of churches will have to deal with an actual lawsuit, but every church should ensure that they set themselves up well."

One pastor on the survey offered his top advice to those considering this ministry: "Please do this. It's not expensive, and it's no more liable to litigation risk than any other ministry."

There's no way to avoid risk altogether in our litigious society. But there are ways to set up the church well. The Church Cares initiative offers resources to help churches do that (see Thechurchcares.com). These resources include template policies, written in part by an experienced legal expert and pastor, that churches can adapt.

In addition, there are some common legal suggestions worth considering as you implement (or expand on) a mental health ministry, such as being sure to articulate specific faith beliefs in your church's governing documents. These are outlined in appendix 1 at the back of the book.

How much does it cost to have a mental health ministry?

A common topic people asked about on the survey was the financial side of having an in-house mental health ministry. Just as there are dozens of ways of setting up such a ministry, there are dozens of answers to "How much does it cost?" It all depends on what type of ministry the church hopes to add.

A church that trains volunteers in lay listening through The Church Cares and refers more challenging cases out to professionals with no financial aid will incur almost no additional costs. A church that creates a full-service counseling center with multiple new employees (licensed therapists, administrators, and so on) and a new building will incur extensive costs.

As you might imagine, there are many options between those two extremes. One of the benefits of adding the trained helper and lay listener levels of the church triangle is that a church can add significant capacity for care with potentially minimal cost.

Let's briefly look at two of the key factors that may add cost along with common solutions.

Adding a Coordinator

Many churches organize this ministry (like most others) under the oversight of a pastor or staff member while the actual work is done by volunteers. The key difference with this ministry is that, ideally, a church should have a central coordinator who fills the intake role, as described in chapter 4 and chapter 7. It takes a specific skill set to funnel people to the right level of care. The more robust the program, the more likely church leaders are to pay a coordinator for a certain number of hours per week.

Adding a Clinician or Paying for Referred Care

Cost is one of the main reasons people who are referred to professionals never receive care. On our survey, more than one-third of church leaders (36 percent) said their church provides substantial help with the cost when parishioners are referred to professional mental health care, either by offering free or low-cost licensed counseling within the church or via a substantial fund for external professionals. Even among small churches with fewer than one hundred members, a significant ratio (29 percent) said they offer this sort of robust help.

When including those who offer a lesser amount of financial help, well over half (57 percent) of all churches offered some form of aid.[8]

Finding Creative Solutions

According to our research, churches often find that the Lord provides creative solutions to help pay for extra costs and make professional care more affordable for church members. For example, it's common for churches to form innovative partnerships with licensed professionals. Churches may offer space to Christian clinicians, with the expectation that the clinician see a specified number of clients at a major discount because of the savings from overhead expenses.

This was a common example offered on the survey: "See if there is an organization you can partner with at a reduced rate, making professional counseling accessible for your church members."

Consider Bartering Services

On the survey, a pastor with a mental health ministry offered this advice: "Fundraise for a professional mental health nonprofit or group so they can offer free counseling and resources to those who need it. Develop a partnership."

In one interview, the director of a large Christian counseling center explained his method of partnering with churches and donors to offset expenses:

> We work with many churches that offer space to our therapists one or more days a week. We don't take insurance

and are solely private pay. All our therapists work on a sliding scale, but they can't take on so many low-paying clients that they're struggling. So we mostly do scholarships. We find donors who want to provide funds and ask churches to reach out to their own donors or set aside part of their budget for this. Our standard is that in ten sessions, our therapists can usually get someone from crisis to at least stable. If someone needs financial help, the usual arrangement is for the client to pay $25 while the church or the foundation pays $100.

Generally speaking, within every parish, there is someone who wants to be of service, maybe in an anonymous way, but doesn't know this is a need. The pastors now keep an eye out, and because there are so many people who have been impacted by the mental health crisis, it's simpler than you might think to find people who will provide financial help.

Moving Beyond the Questions—and to the Solutions

Ultimately, we hope you can see the opportunities behind the questions posed in this chapter and that you are coming to solutions that fit your church and community. That way, the next time someone asks you, "Will it work?" you can say with confidence, "Yes!"

6

Best Practices in Mental Health Ministry

Legal, Ethical, and Leadership Guidelines for Churches

Smart people are a dime a dozen. What matters is the ability to think different ... to think out of the box.

WALTER ISAACSON

From its earliest days, the slogan of International Business Machines Corporation (IBM) was one word: "Think." IBM was a large, established company with a traditional way of doing things, even as leaders in the computing space.

Then, in 1997, the upstart company Apple launched their own slogan: "Think different."

Not only was the upstart poking at the old guard, it was also declaring an important truth. Just thinking isn't enough, because our thoughts usually repeat what we already know. To change something, we have to "think different."

Suddenly, Apple was everywhere. Within a year, its stock price had tripled.[1] A decade later, the company had indeed launched something very different: the iPhone. Soon a new digital ecosystem had evolved, one that most of us live in every day.

Thinking differently led to an entirely new normal.

Churches today must do the same. This chapter promotes thinking differently so we can absorb and implement the best practices of other forward-thinkers. Remember the map analogy? These are the best practices of those who have been exploring these oceans and have learned how to get there and back.

The content is organized around five themes:

1. **Ministry practices:** Thinking through a philosophy that will guide a church's efforts around mental health
2. **Referral practices:** Knowing when to refer and how to continue to walk alongside a person who needs support
3. **Ethical practices:** Maintaining confidentiality and acquiring informed consent
4. **Legal and insurance practices:** Making necessary adjustments to church governing documents and liability insurance
5. **Leadership guidelines:** Ensuring sufficient training and mental health practices for leaders

Our hope is that you will take these lessons, apply your creativity and judgment, and decide on the approach that honors the unique characteristics of your community and the vision you have for your church.

Theme 1: Ministry Practices

Here are some best practices to help integrate mental health ministry into the life and mission of the church.

View mental health ministry as essential to the ultimate mission.

Mental health ministry supports and sustains the primary mission of the church. Churches thrive when care, discipleship, missions, and evangelism are part of the church's DNA.

This is why many churches with mental health ministries provide their services for free for church members. (Often, this is a lay counseling type of service, but it may include professional care as well.)

Many leaders we surveyed echoed the sentiment of this care pastor: "The elders determined that this is a discipleship ministry, so it should be free to the congregants just as it would be if they walked into a discipleship class or a small group."

Keeping an eye on the ultimate mission helps this ministry stay in the right position. As a pastor and a psychologist, Fuller Seminary's Siang-Yang Tan is highly invested in having churches create mental health strategies. He also offered this caution:

> Mental and spiritual health overlap, but they will only be completely in sync in the world to come. We must put our spiritual well-being and our depth of relationship with Jesus Christ as the number one priority. Mental, emotional, and even physical health are important but are not *the* most important thing. We can be spiritually mature yet still have

obsessive-compulsive disorder or bipolar disorder, and God's grace is sufficient. Yes, we should try to relieve suffering, but we should also be careful not to elevate mental and emotional health to be the number one priority.

Incorporate mental health ministry as part of discipleship and evangelism.

Churches with thriving care ministries almost universally urged church leaders to see mental health ministry not as being in competition with discipleship and evangelism but as being central to it—and then organizing it as such. Mental health ministries are most beneficial when they focus not on feeling good but on becoming godly.

When Jeff and I (Shaunti) conducted a marriage event at one small church, the founding pastor showed us around their campus, including a gym where they held youth events and a pickleball court that members of the community were welcome to use. They were also about to open a mental health clinic where they were offering on-site space to Christian counselors.

He said, "Our public statement talks about offering affordable, biblical, and professional mental health services. People who aren't looking for Jesus come here and find that Jesus has been looking for them. We have been doing that through pickleball and community fairs, and now we're doing it through mental health. The local church should be leading the way in this—or at least get in the game."

Ron Deal, a well-known leader in the Christian marriage space and coauthor of *The Mindful Marriage*, emphasized a vital truth in this arena: marriage needs are intertwined with mental health needs, and both are important for care and discipleship. As he put it, "Some of the key practices in improving your marriage and strengthening your mental health are also the best discipleship tools. If I put on self-control with my spouse or surrender myself in sexuality, it means that I have to manage *me* in response to you. Relationships are a refining fire that help grow us up into Christ; they are one of God's best discipleship tools."

Look for ways your mental health ministry can be a solution for the community.

Churches that saw their mental health ministry as part of outreach often had many opportunities come to them. One church leader in a major metro area described how government and school district policies had often created barriers to churches. But after his church began offering mental health services at all levels of the church triangle, more and more people in the community began coming in the doors. Where were all these people coming from?

As it turned out, the local government and local clinicians were so overwhelmed that they had begun asking help seekers if they were open to a "Christian faith approach to mental health." The church leader chuckled as he told us:

> We reached out to the government and offered other help if they wanted it, and eventually the city leaders said, "You know, we need to do better working with the faith community." I was laughing to myself: *Really? You think?* That was the beginning of a major shift. Now I'm the co-chair of the faith collaborative for the entire county. I train

government social workers on how to work with religious clients. I step into secular places and talk about the benefits of faith. And I get to open some eyes when I tell school boards and social workers, "I hope you are inclusive toward people of faith."

Use the available technology to facilitate ministry.

I think we can all agree: most of us now think with our thumbs. Digital technology is a huge part of how people access and respond to information, needs, and opportunities.[2] Since this is part of our new world, the church must be there too.

During the COVID-19 shutdown, most churches magnificently rose to the occasion, rapidly learning how to live stream services. It's easy to forget that in the months before the shutdown, most people had never participated in a video call, attended a virtual worship service, or participated in a live stream webinar. Today those things are seamlessly integrated into our lives when we work remotely, are sick at home, or participate in training while the kids are upstairs in bed.

To facilitate and build a care ministry, we *must* add a digital dimension to the way we think about human care. We can accelerate the number of lay volunteers through training options that don't require everyone to be in the fellowship hall at 7 p.m. on a Thursday night.

I (Shaunti) recently discovered that an old friend had gone through lay counseling training and was preparing to help her church start a mental health ministry. The pastor/licensed therapist who trained her lived on the other side of the country. Of course, I had to talk to him! Here's what he told me:

> We do this training both online and in person. I started in 2006 and thought we would stop in a few years since we're not a big church, but every year we got fifty to a hundred people, so we just kept going. And now, via video, anyone can participate. The vast majority of people who go through the training don't go to our church. There are people problems everywhere. I'm glad to be able to help plant these seeds in other places.

We also heard that digital engagement with those in need can be a great entry point for in-person care. Some people who seek help online grow to trust the church and eventually become connected with small groups, support groups, or the congregation itself.

As you think about what your mental health ministry will look like, be sure to include a digital dimension.

Connect to a network that can help.

So how *can* you digitally reach those in need? One best practice is not to try to build something from scratch but to connect with a group that already has mechanisms to help you.

As mentioned in chapter 4, The Church Cares offers a great option through our partnership with 7 Cups, one of the world's largest peer-to-peer chat-based support systems. Here's an example of how this technology might work for you.

Imagine that your church has ten people trained as lay listeners. Now imagine that Amber, a thirty-nine-year-old occasional church attender, reaches out to a pastor for help. She's grappling with anxiety and a desire to control everything her husband and teenage daughter do. It's starting to drive her daughter away, and her husband has asked Amber to talk to someone. You might think about funneling Amber to a lay listener who can meet her at church once a week. That's a good option.

But now consider some additional details: perhaps Amber works a challenging schedule as a nurse, and finding time to meet is difficult. Also, she's just plain reluctant to have these conversations; she doesn't think she has a problem. She thinks her husband and daughter are the problem! But she's an avid social media user and has plenty of time and inclination to chat online. One of your lay listeners, Bekka, is also active online and says she'd be glad to connect with Amber, including via 7 Cups.

Amber and Bekka both sign in via your church's 7 Cups page and begin a conversation via text over the next few weeks. This isn't a once-a-week meeting but ongoing listening that's much more organic. And there's additional support if Bekka needs it. For example, if Bekka is stumped by something Amber says, an AI helper pops up to suggest a direction. Bekka can't just copy and paste the AI text (the system doesn't allow that), but the system acts as a coach to help her respond when needed. And if there are any signals that Amber is in a danger zone for issues that a lay listener can't handle (like potentially self-harming), the system flags that, and Bekka will be prompted to connect Amber to one of the mental health professionals your church recommends.

Can you see how this technology would expand your church's care for those in need while also allowing for connections far beyond your church? What if, in a different scenario, Amber isn't even an attender of the church? Perhaps she searched on Google or the 7 Cups system for counselors in her area, and your church (which is listed as part of The Church Cares) came up. Perhaps Bekka creates a relationship with Amber for a few weeks through the online chat, invites her to church, and Amber and her family decide to check it out.

Digital care like this is a huge part of the future of outreach to those in need. Even basic steps will extend your church into the culture and help people in the culture find their way to your church.

Use your space as a resource.

Not long ago, Jeff and I (Shaunti) were speaking at a Friday date-night event at a small church in a large city. As the pastor walked us out afterward, we went past a room that was overflowing with noise and laughter. We glimpsed at least fifty people seated around in groups.

He said, "That's the local AA meeting. They needed a place to meet as they grew, and we thought this was a way we could connect with the community. Most of the folks in this group have never been inside a church before, but they are really open. A representative from the church welcomes them each week, and we share elements of the gospel. Because they have a little familiarity with our space, it's easier for them to explore coming to church here on Sunday."

One of the resources many churches have to offer is space that can be used for ministry during the week. While some churches already use every nook and cranny of their building for schools, programs, and food pantries, others have room available. When you take stock of the resources available to help you further your mental health ministry goals, make sure to consider any available space and how it might be used.

Ensure the process is full of grace.

One of the frequent cautions we heard from church leaders who had successful mental health ministries was this: "Take stock of whether your church—and especially the lay helpers—can show the grace hurting people need."

As one pastor said, "People are broken, whether in public or in private. Knowing that their pastors and church members see them with grace and love helps them realize that God receives the real them with grace and love."

Another pastor, who is also a licensed clinician, added this challenge: "People sometimes think the solution to brokenness is to just try harder, read your Bible more, pray more. But that won't bring transformation. Salvation is not a finish line. It's a starting line. Moving toward mental and emotional health must be viewed as a *process*, and it's essential that people are allowed to go through that process without judgment."

Theme 2: Referral Practices

Here are some best practices to help your church be most effective when it comes to referring out.

Remember that referring goes beyond licensed clinicians.

Although we generally speak of *referring* as the process of enlisting a licensed mental health specialist, there are many other types of referrals. A person worn out from insomnia needs a sleep study. A person in deep depression should be referred to a physician to discuss medication. A person who has adopted a child dealing with the aftereffects of trauma needs to be connected with specialized ministries and other families who have gone through the same thing.

All levels of the church CARE triangle (including clinicians) need to keep their eyes open for lay listener and trained helper lifelines within the church and help the person reach out for them. Although unlicensed helpers can develop supportive relationships with those they're caring for, they still can't be the only relational care within the church. Instead, caregivers must help the person transition to people who *can* walk alongside them for the long term—usually people who are part of groups and communities within the church. All caregivers should be frequently reminded of the relevant classes, groups, and ministries within the church in order to be aware of the options and help people plug in and make friends.

And the church can do a lot to help foster these friendships. One pastor of a midsize church said, "The best thing we have ever done for the health of our church is offer free babysitting for church members the first Friday of every month so couples can have a date night or go out for dinner with another couple. It costs money up front, but it saves way more in the long term. We've been doing this for years now, and the whole church is invested because we all see the impact."

Yes, "date night" is a mental health ministry!

Refer to Local Chapters of Moms' Groups

Moms of young children are often at higher risk for mental health issues,[3] with single moms having even higher levels of stress. We know that supportive relationships are helpful in alleviating this stress.[4] There are many Christian groups that offer fellowship and support. For example, MomCo (formerly called MOPS) has chapters in thousands of churches. Women often meet weekly, going through a curriculum and just sharing life together. This is often the most supportive relationship base that moms of young children in a given church will have. Consider referring moms to these groups or starting a chapter in your church.

Know when to refer to a licensed clinician.

As a church builds lay levels of mental health care, it's essential for leaders to think through the triggers for enlisting a licensed professional. You should be aware of the behavioral and verbal markers that raise questions, know when to get advice, and decide in advance what situations require escalation to a clinician. What level of complexity warrants a referral? After how many meetings with the lay volunteer or the pastor should someone be referred out? Are there specific issues, such as ongoing substance abuse or suicidal ideation, that require a clinician?

Once those decisions have been made, everyone in your ministry, from the pastor to the lay listener, must know the church's protocol. In most cases, the caregiver consults with the coordinator, who makes the ultimate evaluation and decision.

Here are some common thresholds at which many experts say pastoral or lay caregiving should give way to a highly trained professional. (You can see other examples in appendix 1 online.)

- suicidal ideation, thoughts, or actions
- current chemical addictions

- violence or threats
- emotional dysregulation (loss of control of behavior—shouting, breaking things, reckless or dangerous actions)
- adolescent failure to thrive (absence of friends, loss of interest or ambition, disconnection from school or other activities, self-harm)
- childhood patterns of behavior at home or school that are significantly outside expected ranges

A number of church leaders mentioned a positive ripple effect when it comes to referring to clinicians who are physically available at the church. One pastor advised on the survey, "By having a trained professional on-site, we found that people are more willing to attend counseling. You will notice a significant lightening of your load of recurring individual meetings with parishioners."

Just remember: referral is intended to extend the ministry of the church, not to free the church from the opportunity for continued ministry. When parents of a child diagnosed with a conduct disorder are referred to a clinician, they need a caring church more, not less. When a couple in crisis is referred to a marriage and family therapist, they need a couples' small group more, not less. Each time someone is referred, it's beneficial to establish a way for the church to be a place of continued healing for that person.

Get Advice from a Clinician

We received this advice on the survey for any church that's building a mental health ministry: "Get all the guidance you can from mental health professionals. Especially, get insight on where the line is—where pastoral counseling issues end and mental health issues begin."

Establish a way of vetting each outside provider.

Referring out to external providers—whether licensed clinicians, certified biblical counselors, or certified coaches—requires a means of vetting providers to be confident they will provide both competent and biblical counsel that honors church teaching.

Years ago, I (Shaunti) spent nearly a year trying to encourage an old friend to work on her marriage to a good man rather than leave due to a childhood trauma reaction. A pastor gave me a referral for a Christian therapist, and my friend finally agreed to see her.

Her email describing the first session was one line: "My counselor said marriage isn't for everybody."

As you can imagine, I was devastated and furious—and so was the pastor who gave the referral. He had received no feedback from previous clients, so he assumed this "Christian counselor" would be supportive of marriage. Thankfully, my friend later recommitted her life to Christ and her husband. But the incident provided a lesson echoed by pastors on the survey:

- "Vet your referrals very thoroughly; *know* them."
- "Do your due diligence with coaches and counselors. Be sure to vet them all."
- "Get references and recommendations about any counselor or service before using them."

- "Be very careful who you refer your people to; seek references from Christ-centered/gospel-centered leaders."

The need for competent, trustworthy professionals is one reason to connect with referral networks—for example, some denominations or dioceses have a network of recommended counselors in various regions. (See appendix 2 at Thechurchcares.com for examples of referral networks and many other resources.) Then build a relationship with a few professionals. As mentioned in chapter 3, this will also help get your people in more quickly.

Continue to care for those who are referred out.

As noted, one of the shifts needed today involves finding ways to stay in touch with and continue to care for people who are referred to external clinicians.

In the current mental health culture, clinicians work in relative isolation. The working relationship is limited to the clinician and the client. The community of supporters who might strengthen clinical outcomes—and who will remain in relationship long after therapy is over—is seldom consulted. But it doesn't have to be this way. Pastors can build relationships with the clinicians who are in their network. Assignments and tasks given to the client by the clinician can be shared with the pastor, coordinator, and caregiver so the church can support and strengthen the clinical efforts.

Some mental health professionals may be reluctant to "share care" and may be concerned that advice from the church might undo the work they're doing. This is all the more reason that communication between professionals and the church/community be ongoing, so that any misunderstandings can be recognized before they create problems and so that boundaries can be respected and clarified as needed.

Other professionals, by contrast, will be delighted to have the church walk alongside those in need, especially since clinicians are usually prohibited from developing more personal connections. This is particularly true for chronic mental health issues and clinical and personality disorders. Having the community present and active in a support role throughout sustained treatment may be an important part of care.

Multiple church leaders and therapists also mentioned that churches could fill the important role of helping to coordinate care. One pastor, who is also a licensed therapist, put it this way:

> In mental health, just like in medical health, we have a problem of siloed care. Creating fluid communication is critical if we want to care for the whole person—and do it for more than just a few weeks during therapy. After treatment, the person needs to be reintegrated into a nonclinical system that can support them! And the more there can be some sort of guidance from the church and back to the church, the more effective treatment will be—and the more effective all the help will be.

Theme 3: Ethical Practices

Here are some best practices to ensure good boundaries for both the ministry and those being helped.

Stay in your lane.

When we sought advice from highly trained professionals on the issue of how the church can ethically and safely step in to help with the mental health crisis, we consistently heard this counsel: "Stay in your lane." In other words, stay within the scope of your training and calling.

For pastors, this doesn't mean that mental health isn't your lane and spiritual health is. These two areas overlap inextricably. It does mean that when you address mental health issues such as anxiety, trauma reactivity, or eating disorders, you keep focused on your role and skill set as a pastoral counselor instead of thinking that you somehow need to become a clinical therapist, psychiatrist, or neuropsychologist.

After all, pastoral counsel is what this person needs from you! They need your help to trust God and cope with fear. They need your encouragement that they can, indeed, walk through this difficult season and come out healthy on the other side. Of course, you can and should be informed on the latest research and share tested strategies as part of your work with someone in need. But just keep in mind that this person can get clinical assessments and dispassionate advice on empirically proven trauma approaches from clinicians, but in most cases, they can't get pastoral care from those clinicians. Your lane is essential.

For all categories of caregivers, including licensed therapists, it's vital to honor and stick with the unique calling you've been given. We can all learn additional skills and add them to our toolbox. But to be ethical and safe, we do need to know when we've reached the limit of what our tools are intended to do.

Maintain confidentiality.

Most of us have parroted the classic line from *The Princess Bride* (complete with accent), "You keep using that word. I do not think it means what you think it means."[5] When it comes to the word *confidentiality*, there are some similar issues!

In a counseling context, confidentiality means that the listener is bound by professional ethics codes and laws that define and restrict how content is managed. A clinician must protect the client's interest and doesn't share information about a client without their permission. Unless this information puts someone in danger, the content of a counseling session is considered protected communication. That doesn't mean clinicians can't reveal counseling content; it means that the clients are the ones to decide who has access to that information and what is revealed, as all confidential content is the "property" of the client.

Details are *held* by the professional, who can't disclose any information about care or treatment, *unless* the client requests it to be shared.[6] However, if the client does request it, the professional is ethically obligated to do so.

These rules pertain to licensed professionals and are defined by federal and state laws and the ethics of various mental health professions. Pastors have a different set of freedoms and obligations regarding confidential material. Lay caregivers are neither clinicians nor pastors. Therefore, to prevent confusion and misunderstanding, the specific rules regarding confidentiality must be determined by each church, defined and described in their policy, emphasized during training, disclosed to all participants at the onset of care, and discussed and enforced in an ongoing way in the ministry.

Regardless of the specific policy, keeping the confidences of the person seeking help is important both for ethical reasons and for effective ministry. One pastor offered this as his top advice: "Client confidentiality is mandatory in order to build trust."

Specific confidentiality policies will depend on the goals of the church. For example, some churches have a completely hands-off policy, either because of the laws of the state (for licensed clinicians) or because of the preference of the pastor, or both. One licensed therapist who works in a church put it this way:

> Privacy is a big issue I run into. We have laws that prevent us as clinicians from communicating back to the church leadership. In the case of our church, the pastor initiated a clear rule that the church wants to know nothing about what's going on. He wants to protect the counseling time to make sure something doesn't bleed over into being publicly known that might cost the client their job or something.

This church chose to keep a strong boundary between the practice of therapy and the practice of ministry. Although these types of problems are rare, some issues may indeed be averted by having this separation. Yet other problems might be *created* by the community caregiver and pastoral team not knowing appropriate details of care.

This is why other churches, by contrast, want to be able to get the help seeker's permission to stay in touch and walk alongside them in the process. (We describe how to do that a bit more in a moment.) Wanting that flexibility is one reason why some mental health caregivers choose to be biblical counselors or coaches rather than licensed counselors. While confidentiality is important regardless, the unlicensed roles provide additional flexibility, including being more personally involved in the life of the client.

Many ethics codes for licensed clinicians make space for "treatment teams," or collaborators in a person's care, such as a pastor and a physician. The code requires that the client have full awareness of the members of the team, the type of information shared, and access to information. In all cases, the best interest of the client is protected.[7]

Dr. Kristen Kansiewicz, an authority in clinical counseling and pastoral care, made this comment: "If you are a counselor and you obtain authorization from the client, you can reach out to their pastor. Pastors, you can reach out to counselors (who will at that point have to have the client sign a release before returning your call)."[8] Trust and collaboration between clergy and clinicians are paramount in caring for the vulnerable.

One church pastor, who is also a licensed marriage and family therapist, described the way his church builds relationships between clinicians, church members, and the church care team:

> We create an agreement between the person, the counseling agency, and the church. We tell the person, "Nikki, we love you and we're going to support you, and we want to journey with you as well. Are you willing to share with us along the way? Is it okay for us to talk to your counselor? We won't be hearing personal details, but we want their guidance."
>
> For example, I want to be able to ask the counselor, "Would it be helpful for Nikki if she had a mentor who

> could work with her on this or that issue?" So we're given guidance without personal details. Then we bring a lay helper alongside Nikki to establish trust. We want Nikki to be able to share her story and have a companion who personally cares, in addition to a therapist.

Both the church and the clinic seek the same thing: security that the person in need is respected and helped in the most effective way, while at the same time following all relevant laws, policies, and best-practice guidelines. When problems occur, in most cases, the issue is not the policy but the fact that the policy doesn't exist or that it isn't taken seriously. Churches can feel secure in this arena when policies are defined, described, maintained, and followed as well as possible.

Think through what communication is allowed within the church.

Sometimes it's best if pastors don't know certain things. Take finances, for example. It's often the case that pastors don't know what each member gives in annual tithing, since that could impact the way they do ministry. Some information divulged in private between a help seeker and a caregiver is best left outside the pastor's awareness.

We're not talking about issues that must be reported according to ethical guidelines. If a help seeker says, "Please don't tell anyone, but I'm having an affair and I'm planning to leave my husband," such a topic is beyond the level of a lay caregiver's role. The appropriate response would be "I can't keep that information secret. Remember, the informed consent we discussed at the beginning said that there are areas beyond what we can address here and require advanced consultation. We need to talk to the church coordinator. I'm glad to be with you as you tell the story. But I'm simply not trained to provide support in this situation."[9]

It's a different situation when the church is tempted to seek information from the caregiver about the content of their conversations. Imagine a pastor approaching a lay counselor who is working with Diana, a married church member. The pastor asks the caregiver, "I know you're seeing Diana Johnson. We are considering asking her husband, Tyler, to serve as a deacon. Biblically, we need to know about the stability of a deacon's marriage. Has she said anything that would make us hesitant about this appointment?"

Such a topic must remain closed and off-limits. When trust and boundaries are disrespected, it injures the integrity of the church and its leadership. If pastors want to learn this information, they need to speak to the person directly and not use the lay caregiver as a third-party informant. In this example, they would need to ask the candidate and/or his wife directly, or they could ask the candidate to provide letters of support from people who can speak to his marriage.

Of course, there are limited times when confidentiality *must* be broken, such as when it's clear that somebody could get hurt.

Have clear written informed consent.

The key to all these ethical issues is to ensure that the help seeker fully understands and agrees to the type and process of care. There must be *written* agreements, signed by both parties—both to ensure that all key points are understood and agreed to and to protect the church.

Three areas were frequently mentioned as essential to include in an informed consent document.

First, it's important to get full buy-in from the help seeker for external communication with the therapist. If there's any sense of coercion ("Well, they're paying for it, so I guess I have to agree to it even if it makes me uncomfortable"), it could *add* to the hurt and pain instead of bringing healing. (Ethics codes also emphasize that paying for someone's services doesn't entitle the benefactor to know the content of those counseling sessions.)

Second, informed consent is essential for any church program that includes care from laypeople instead of (or in addition to) professionals. The help seeker needs to fully understand and acknowledge what this care involves (for example, listening, compassion, or helping the person think things through), what it doesn't involve (for example, it's not professional counseling, advice, or psychotherapy), and that they are voluntarily participating.

Third, the paperwork often lists the process and requirements so the expectations are clear. For example, the document might say that the church will provide eight weekly sessions of lay counseling for free but that if the client misses two weeks in a row, they may need to withdraw from the program so someone who is more invested can take their spot.

Theme 4: Legal and Insurance Practices

In appendix 1, we share some specifics about how to set up a church well for legal and insurance protection as the church moves into mental health ministry. Here are a few other best practices to consider.

Do what you can to protect the church legally, but avoid decisions based on fear.

Although most pastors move forward in mental health ministry despite the risks, those who are particularly concerned about legal and liability concerns tend to do less in this arena. Many leaders whose networks, dioceses, or churches had been caught up in prior abuse lawsuits were particularly sensitive to this concern. On the survey, one ministry director shared this regret: "Our mental health ministry is allowed to have licensed, insured professionals give presentations, but our priest forbade us from having an actual accompaniment ministry because of liability."

A leader in the biblical counseling space also pointed out that a church should get good legal counsel based on the laws of their state if they include licensed clinicians as part of their strategy. He said, "People think, 'If I'm licensed, I can protect the church.' It's actually the opposite. When you have a license, you have dual authority over you. You have your own biblical convictions, but you also have the licensing board that governs you. A common issue is about views of sexuality. If you're licensed and in the church, you have a fine line you have to walk."

He described his church's biblical counseling model. "We have to be legally wise. All counselors in our church carry some sort of liability insurance. For any church with a formal counseling ministry, we suggest extra coverage for each person. We also require counselees to sign a consent form sharing the scope of the ministry, limits on confidentiality, and so on. If someone becomes disgruntled, nothing will keep them from suing, but in court, those signed documents saying the help seeker is voluntarily participating are usually enough."

Know what to do if something awful happens.

Even with full vetting and the efforts to screen and protect, horrible things can happen. We've talked about how to protect the church from lawsuits, accusations, and legal frays. Tragically, there are times when people who submit to the church end up deeply injured. Consider, for example, the sexual abuse scandals that have brought unspeakable damage to victims as well as churches.

There are many ministries that exist to help churches protect themselves (before tragedy) and to help churches wisely and courageously address a crisis (during and after tragedy). One such resource is PastorServe, which offers consultation, mentorship, and support for pastors and churches facing complicated challenges.[10]

One thing every church should do in advance is consider this sobering question: How will we handle it if a particular accusation (for example, an accusation of sexual abuse) is made? This is something many churches and denominations have grappled with. No matter how a church decides to handle the specifics, it's vital to consider *in advance* how to approach any accusations with Christlike humility and a willingness to listen. If a church hasn't thought it through, there may be a tendency to circle the wagons during the initial response. That's a harmful pattern that can only cause pain—and has indeed led to "church hurt" when it's handled poorly. But if there's any potential validity to the accusation, church leaders must be prepared to come alongside the victim in sincere care, remorse for the pain caused, and a desire to help bring healing and restoration.

Theme 5: Leadership Guidelines

Finally, here are some best practices for healthy leadership as your church builds its mental health ministry.

Keep yourself healthy.

Mental health starts at the top. Although the survey and the interviews didn't specifically address the mental health of pastors themselves, the topic came up frequently. In part because pastors walk through these issues, just like everyone else does. (In a 2021 survey of Protestant pastors, Lifeway Research found that 26 percent said they had struggled with a mental illness of some kind.[11]) Many leaders emphasized that ultimately the mental health of the leader, and their willingness to work to be healthy themselves, has a great deal to do with the overall transparency, care, and health of a church body.

A study by Kristen Kansiewicz found that the number of friends a pastor had was related to many other variables that impacted their effectiveness in ministry. Nearly 40 percent of pastors had two or fewer close friends, with 9 percent of pastors saying that they had none.[12]

A pastor and denominational leader offered this summary: "Until we start demystifying these issues with mental health, we will not have a healthy church, especially if the pastor isn't healthy himself. Because if he's not healthy, his wife isn't healthy. His kids aren't healthy. Because Daddy is paying too much attention to the church and not the family. It starts at the top. But if the leader can talk about what he has suffered and seek help—if he can be open about it—everyone knows it's okay. As pastors, we're passionate about helping people, and that has to include ourselves."

Multiple leaders pointed out that resources exist for pastoral mental health. As one advised, "A pastor's denomination, church network, or diocese probably has a list of mental health resources for leaders—and if they don't, ask for one. Because this is something everyone is looking at right now."

Talk About Mental Health from the Stage

Many church leaders stressed the importance of pastors mentioning mental health issues and the church's mental health ministry from the pulpit. One pastor told us, "We see that helps even when people don't actually engage with the ministry. On their own, they call therapists, and then I get an email saying how our mental health ministry has really helped them. And I'm like [laughing], 'We didn't do anything!'"

Train well.

On the survey's open-ended request for advice, one of the top comments was the recommendation that a church invest in a strong training program. Solid vetting of volunteers—and good training and supervision for them—is one solution to the common concern that a pastor isn't sure which caregivers they can trust. Training helps them build a stable of those they *can* trust.

As noted, good training for either trained helpers (such as lay counselors) or lay listeners will emphasize, as one lay counselor put it, "ensuring that everyone learns how to stick with their appropriate scope and then ask great questions. That's part of what we're trained to do. We become journalists, in a way, and we help the person open up to get out what's truly on their heart. When we ask those questions and let them come to self-discovery, it unlocks things for them. The process empowers them to figure out what they need to do on their own."

Additional training can be offered during supervision times. One example might be knowing what to do in a large-scale crisis. Tragically, it's all too common for people in a community to witness or respond to a traumatic situation such as a natural disaster or a school shooting. One key tool, called a critical incident stress debriefing (CISD), doesn't require a licensed therapist, just someone with training in taking people through the process. When done well, it can reduce the risk of developing trauma symptoms and other mental health issues.

None of these practices will be perfect (as noted, licensed counselors aren't perfect either). But as you implement the strategies that work for you, in the *way* they work for you, you and your people will be far more confident as you step into this area of ministry.

PART 2

Preparing People for Mental Health Ministry

Part 2 Introduction

Grace and *love* are such beautiful words. The idea that anything of goodness would be granted to you and me without merit, simply because of love—what a gift. And the idea that we would be infused with God's power so we can extend that love and grace to others—now that's world changing!

Grace, love, and God's transforming power are the primary distinctions between care ministry and clinical therapy. While professional mental health care offers excellent service and treatment, it is not designed to deliver grace and love, nor does it (as a discipline) call on God's power for healing. Therapy can reduce painful symptoms, and God can, of course, be at work anywhere. But therapy cannot offer meaning and purpose. The church can.

A common benediction at the end of some church services says it all: "May the grace of the Lord Jesus Christ, the love of God, and the fellowship of the Holy Spirit be with you all" (2 Corinthians 13:14, NLT). As we think about people who are hurting and the caring church, we will use those words as more than platitudes or encouraging thoughts. We seek to make those words the real experience when hurting people come to church.

Part 2 of this book offers a brief journey into the *how* of building a mental health ministry in your church. We'll get to the specifics soon, but first, and most significantly, it's important to establish that a church ministry must start and end with the foundation of grace, love, and God's power to transform lives. As you stand at the helm of the ship, be conscious of always steering according to these truths.

Care Without God's Grace Is Incomplete

In the immediate aftermath of 9/11, when the ruins were still smoking and emergency workers were exhausted, mental health professionals and researchers flooded in to provide volunteer care to the first responders. They intended to help by providing clinical therapeutic interventions and found that help was already there, but in a different form. They discovered a community of support, care, compassion, and love. The researchers wrote:

> In searching for words to describe our experiences . . . we tried out a number of alternatives to "grace" including luck, chance, coincidence, and serendipity. None of these alternatives quite captured our experiences and our sense that certain events may best be conceptualized as unsolicited "gifts" that facilitated our work at the WTC site. So while the term "grace" may seem out of place in the scientific and professional literature, it fits well as a descriptor of some of our experiences as we continue our struggle to understand them.[1]

Professional clinicians might exhibit a type of grace through conduct that is, essentially, common kindness. They genuinely care for those they treat. But one of the most basic components of true healing—a caring, personal relationship—is purposefully absent. Unlike pastors, biblical counselors, and lay caregivers, licensed caregivers are not permitted to have a reciprocal relationship. In order to preserve objectivity, the care is to be unidirectional.

Clinicians offer expertise to reduce painful symptoms. They will not care for the client as a friend. If a single mother's child is diagnosed with a terminal illness, she may go to a clinician to address her grief. The clinician cannot be at the bedside, holding her hand as the child nears death—but the church can. Not only does the church step into that space, it also brings the only thing that can truly make a difference in such a season: the grace and love of Jesus.

A clinician often has affection for clients, and Christian clinicians work to bring God's peace, but affection at a distance can't compete with grace-giving love. Parents love their kids, despite everything that drives them crazy. Friends love and serve one another even when it's hard. The mental health profession can't offer a loving presence, and its model isn't based on grace. But for churches, both are their very heartbeat.

Clinicians and the church have the same goal for people in pain, and they must collaborate in providing support. Yet even though the church and the clinic have parallel tracks in providing care, the clinic's track will stop once the goals of therapy have been met. The church's track runs to the horizon.

Care Without Community Is Incomplete

For growth toward maturity to occur, every person requires community. We won't dive into the specifics of how to build community in this book, but we want to emphasize the need for churches to attend to such a goal. Ninety-six percent of survey takers agreed or somewhat agreed that "a community of believers supporting one another is one of the best ways to foster good mental health inside the church."

Community preexists any type of mental health intervention and follows it. The church is there after therapy ceases.

We know that community is the most important resource for well-being. Even as a clinical psychologist, if I (Jim) could wish for someone in need to have either a great therapist or a great friend, I would pick the friend. We all would.

The church becomes the modality for *relationship*—with God and with others. And those relationships are so crucial for abundant life. As Jesus said, "The thief comes only to steal and kill and destroy; I have come that they may have life, and have it to the full" (John 10:10, NIV).

These relationships are also crucial as the church beckons to those who stand on the periphery or outside the church, wondering if Jesus has any relevance to their feelings of isolation, sadness, or worry. Church leadership expert Carey Nieuwhof told us,

> Many pastors see counseling, relationship building, and pastoral care for the church and community as something that fuels them. They may not initially *want* to release some of that to others—but they become willing to do so because they have too many appointments. The issue is that they often don't have a *system* to make delegation happen. The number one reason most churches never make it past two hundred people is because they don't know how to scale pastoral care. So having a system to do that is essential for the church to reach its potential.

If the church as a community is intended to support all of us in need and reach out to others, and if the church's key "system" is to designate and prepare laypeople to be part of that support and outreach, then we must answer the next question: “How do we do that?”

Leading the Church Toward Care

The following short chapters are written to give pastors (as executives) and coordinators (as managers) the big picture for filling out all levels of the church triangle. The goal is to help you find and prepare lay caregivers to render care for those who are hurting. As such, we will focus on the people, skills, and strategies needed. Some of the concepts covered in these chapters are basic ideas that lay listeners can learn in just a few hours, while others are more advanced ideas that may be taught to trained helpers such as lay counselors.

There are many excellent resources (including those available through The Church Cares and other ministries listed in appendix 2) that dive deep into what lay caregivers need to know—and at some point, the coordinator or some other leader will need to select and implement that training. But right now, all you need is the big picture of what’s required so you know *how* caregivers and coordinators are trained and so you can set the policies and boundaries of your care ministry.

In other words, these chapters are leadership chapters, not clinical training chapters.

What You’ll Learn in Part 2

In the following chapters, we identify the roles needed for this type of ministry, as well as five areas of competence that caregivers will need as they prepare for and step into their ministry on an ongoing basis. These chapters provide an introduction to this content for leaders.

Chapter 7 describes the necessary people and their roles: pastor, coordinator, and lay caregiver. These sections provide more detail about these roles and their key responsibilities so you can set up an effective mental health ministry.

Chapter 8 is about listening. Church caregivers must earn the right to provide care by being great listeners and by helping people in pain understand how to work through their distress and think through their situation *for themselves*, rather than by being great solution providers. Paul encourages us in Romans 12:12 to be "patient in affliction" (NIV). The first skill set to be mastered by the church care community is simply being a calm, caring, and listening presence.

Chapter 9 addresses managing emotions, such as fear, discouragement, and anger. You may have witnessed how emotions can become controlling forces in life—a "tail wagging the dog" experience. Much of nonclinical support involves a lay caregiver helping someone to "place the dog in front of the tail."

Chapter 10 focuses on healing relationships, such as those within marriages and families. The space between broken people is one of the most damaging and draining sources of friction and mental health concerns. Lay caregivers help spouses, families, and others understand how to live and interact well in the same space so each person can grow in the image of God and be a blessing, rather than a drain, for the other.

Chapter 11 focuses on addictions and getting free from habits that control us. The gospel has unique power to bring recovery from addiction and address temptation, because the heart of its message is that on our own we are powerless—but we can be utterly changed through God's power. Lay caregivers, as fellow travelers, can help people understand how to lean in to God rather than whatever else they're tempted to depend on.

Chapter 12 is about trauma and grief and being present in the furnace. Life can be hard. Grief and trauma can bend our spine into a painful twist. The Christian journey is meant to help us stand straight. Although some aspects of trauma, in particular, benefit from work with specialized clinicians, a lay caregiver can offer hope and (as described in chapter 8) the ministry of presence and a listening ear. The goal is to help the person acknowledge the painful reality and influence of their story, while not being consumed or crushed by it.

This may seem like an intimidating list of skills to build. But it is vital to note that many people in your congregation or group already have these skills. Mature Christians who are empathetic and calm are good candidates for extra training in listening and how to be present when emotions run high.

Finally, in the **conclusion**, we share some closing thoughts about the opportunity before the church today, including data and evidence about how these types of programs are working.

7

The Necessary People

Getting the Right Team Prepared and in Place

Problems can become opportunities
when the right people come together.

ROBERT SOUTH

Great players are essential for great teams. But they have a lot of help from people who don't wear the uniform. Behind the players are the coaches, and behind the coaches are the executives. These three levels exist in almost every arena—from disaster response units to sports teams to new ministries at a church.

The executive is the first decision maker, the one who says, "The buck stops here." Pastors know that feeling. They make things happen, but they do so by casting the vision and ensuring that other leaders have what they need to carry it out.

Next is the manager who implements the vision and promotes the culture. We refer to this person (or people) as the coordinator(s).

Executives and managers (pastors and coordinators) put great players on the field. John McKissick, the winningest football coach of all time, said, "Coaches don't win games, players do. Players don't lose games, coaches do."[1] Players are the lay caregivers prepared by pastors and coordinators to do the ministry.

As churches create effective, transformative CARE ministry, people with specific skills are needed in each of these roles: the pastor, the coordinator, and the caregiver. Let's define those roles and what skills they entail.

The Pastor

As the visionaries, pastors help create a workable, sustainable, and transformational mental health strategy. They do this in four main ways.

Cast the vision, and empower others to implement it.

The first task of the pastor is leadership and administration. Think of the three *p*'s: purpose, plan, and process. The pastor puts out the call for the person to head the working group (see chapter 4), oversees the development of the church's strategy, makes the final decisions based on the working group's recommendations, creates space for others to conduct the ministry, and ensures that they have the resources they need.

One pastor advised this on the survey:

> Be sure to have a detailed plan in place, with dedicated individuals who are willing to receive necessary training. Take the time to be sure that your volunteers understand the mission. Don't be surprised or disappointed if the outreach begins slowly. A few dedicated participants will be able to

reach others they know are struggling and bring them in if they themselves feel safe. Be sure to educate the parish at large about the efforts in order to reduce the stigma.

The key to the CARE strategy is for the pastor to consider care at all levels. One survey taker offered his top advice to those considering this ministry: "Establish a multitiered, integrated mental health support system that includes trained professionals, pastoral care, and lay counselors/caregivers." (To that, we would add the lower level of the triangle: lay listeners.) And this system will need to be adapted to the unique vision of each pastor and the unique structure and culture of each local church.

For example, one pastor of a small suburban church of about 150 became committed to doing this sort of caring ministry. He came from an addictions background and was attuned to human brokenness, so the community knew this was a place they would be received with open arms. But it also meant the church received many calls for help with addictions, food, shelter, counseling, medical referrals, marital stress, despair, and worry—everything. The church already had a strong small group ministry, so rather than create a unique care ministry, the pastor decided to integrate care skills into each of the small groups. What worked for this small church was not "Sign up for this new ministry," but rather "Everyone is to be trained as a caregiver."

Create the culture.

Pastors see, hear, and engage the needs of the community and the congregation. They inspire others to join the vision and tailor the church's purpose to the needs around them. Ultimately, pastors create culture. They set the standard for others to follow—the tone and the focus. Everything clicks when the congregation is involved, invested, and repeatedly informed of the dream and direction of the ministry.

On the survey, one leader offered this as their top advice: "Preach mental health from the pulpit. Normalize it. Encourage it. Support it. Explain it."

Another pointed out, "The people of your church need and ultimately want the help. So many won't reach out for themselves, but when the church comes alongside them and shows that it's normal to need help, they're more likely to seek and get help."

Building a new culture of care needs to be a shared project, and it works best if the congregation makes the vision its own. We've heard this good news repeatedly from pastors who have launched such a new vision: even parishioners who aren't directly involved are proud to be part of a church that addresses such a clear cultural need. They often become evangelists for the church, telling others that it's a place to connect and receive care. This type of culture is also most likely to provide a place that's perceived as loving and safe by those who are a bit skeptical or who have a past marked by church hurt.

Model vulnerability.

Churches with an effective care culture are almost always led by pastors who take the risk of being personally vulnerable and who translate that to mutual compassion.

The origin of *vulnerability* is Latin—literally "the ability to be wounded." Both churches and secular culture value self-reliance, independence, and invulnerability. We are all like the three-year-old who defiantly says, "I can do it myself." Leading the way in vulnerability and humility means showing that we *can't* do it on our own. Christianity is grounded on the truth that we're all wounded and in need of grace.

To lead people toward mutual compassion and care, pastors must lead them away from subtle tendencies toward pride, self-sufficiency, and autonomy. This requires leaders to directly confront and debunk damaging perceptions that get in the way. One of these damaging messages may sound compassionate but is actually driven by pride: *good Christian folks don't have needs—they help others in need.* This evil is broken when confronted publicly by the pastor, who leads the way in stating that we *all* have needs, that everyone carries pain, and that the church is made up of one imperfect follower of Christ helping another.

Guide toward grace.

When friends care for one another in times of worry, sadness, or unhealthy life patterns, it rarely gets tangled up with theological or psychological squabbles. But once those same patterns are labeled "mental health" related, for some reason, squabbles can indeed arise. This is where the pastor has a vital role to lead the church toward finding biblical balance and showing grace toward differing opinions.

Otherwise, these types of comments tend to proliferate:

- "Clearly, relying on medicine is a crutch and just masks the real issue."
- "Clearly, if you want to be well, you have to take your medicine."
- "Clearly, you need to trust God more."

- "Clearly, your therapist is the professional, and you need to do what they say."
- "Clearly, this is caused by spiritual warfare and a lack of spiritual maturity."
- "Clearly, this is psychological, not a lack of spiritual maturity."

The reality is that mental, emotional, and behavioral issues are messy, and there's a deep need for the church to show grace to others and their strongly held beliefs. In fact, if we take out the word *clearly* (which connotes more certainty than is usually appropriate), each of these statements might be true in a given situation! In this book, as we hope you've noticed, we're trying to help all streams of the church, which means majoring on the majors and not getting into debates or being pulled into different corners representing sincerely held beliefs about theology or psychology.[2] We hope pastors and others will lead their people in doing the same.

This is important not just because we're called to avoid "quarreling over disputable matters" (Romans 14:1, NIV) but because without the church showing humility and grace, people might experience harm instead of help.

It's common for caregivers or care seekers to passionately advocate for a given mental health approach because they've seen how effective that approach is. Yet God doesn't work or lead the same way in every person's life. As long as another approach is consistent with biblical principles, pastors can model and demonstrate humility when others might be led in that direction.

For example, how should we view anxiety? In years past, I (Shaunti) dealt with significant anxiety around flying. My thoughts became panicky as I pictured all the possible horrifying outcomes. We canceled Christmas with Jeff's family one year because I was so panicked at the airport that I literally made myself sick. This only began to change once I felt God challenging me to take seriously His command (through Paul, in Philippians 4:6), "Do not be anxious about anything, but in every situation, by prayer and petition, with thanksgiving, present your requests to God" (NIV).

My situation fit every description of an anxiety disorder and easily would have qualified as a medical issue, deserving of medication. Yet *in my particular case*, I didn't need medicine; I needed to take my anxious thoughts captive, learn to lean on and trust the Lord, and practice a different process of thinking over the next several years.

Yet there are people whose panic strikes them down not just when they're at the airport but when they're pushing a grocery cart in aisle 2, trying to choose between multigrain or wheat bread. That person's panic disorder may indeed need to be addressed medically.

One person we spoke with about these matters has a particularly wide point of view: he's the senior pastor of a large church *and* an experienced clinical psychologist *and* someone whose approach to counseling looks first at the heart and is consistent with many biblical counseling principles. As he put it, "Most problems are not either/or but impact us psychologically, physically, *and* spiritually. When we make a problem primarily something it's not, there's potential for harm."

The Coordinator

As noted in chapter 4, many different types of people can make great coordinators. They may be in the therapeutic world (such as licensed clinicians, certified biblical counselors, or trained coaches), pastoral ministry, discipleship, education, medicine, or dozens of other arenas.

What responsibilities do the coordinators have?

There are four primary tasks for the coordinator (or coordinators) to accomplish: create the team, train the caregivers, supervise/oversee the ministry, and assess/connect help seekers to the right means of care. For the sake of simplicity, we're assuming that the same person does both the care-related/supervision tasks and the managerial/administration tasks. (If a church is relying on an unpaid coordinator, however, we would caution against loading up a clinical expert with administrative tasks that could be done by someone else.)

Create the Team

This is both the easiest task and the hardest. People want to help others, and this is especially true of those who have known the crushing force of life. It's often easy to find lay volunteers for this ministry. The person who is now cancer-free wants to help the person who just got a diagnosis. The former addict wants to help the person who is struggling. The person impacted by parental divorce wants to help the teenager who is going through a family split.

The line to be a part of the team forms quickly. A greater challenge is to vet caregivers who might not be ready, who are prone to speak more than listen, who lack depth in Christian maturity, who seek to help as a means of avoiding their own pain, or who are motivated by strong opinions about what has helped them and are certain of what everyone else should do to become "as healthy and healed as yours truly!" (Yikes.)

Train the Caregivers

The level and intensity of lay training will depend on the level and intensity of need to be met. The middle level of the church CARE triangle, trained helpers, includes those who go through longer and more involved training. This includes people like Stephen Ministers, those receiving mental health coach certification through the American Association of Christian Counselors, certified biblical counselors, lay counselors, and other fairly robust roles.

The lower level of the CARE triangle, lay listeners, requires basic training in at least these key sets of skills.

Effective listening is, by far, the most important skill set for *all* levels of care. We will provide more details about how to listen well in the next chapter. But more important than knowing what to say is knowing how and when to *not* say anything. By listening, the caregiver communicates a great deal. They communicate that the other person is important. They communicate understanding. They communicate an active, engaged presence. They communicate that the person's concern is indeed as complicated as it feels to them. They communicate that platitudes and trite clichés are neither welcomed nor delivered.

Another skill set that coordinators must teach caregivers is how to use the Bible—and how not to. They must be trained to avoid proof-texting, in which a verse is taken out of context and applied as a simplistic "You should do *X*" answer to complicated circumstances. The listener must also be intentional about elevating a person in pain rather than suppressing them with church-delivered guilt that matches the weight of the shame or other emotions they're already carrying. This was a refrain we heard frequently on the survey, as reflected in the words of one ministry director at a large church: "Always keep prayer, listening, and accompaniment *without judgment* at the center of your ministry."

An additional skill that should be built involves guiding someone toward trusting and leaning in to God in difficult circumstances. In our human nature, we often seek to relieve all painful emotions. But what if these experiences—especially the ones that weigh us down—are meant to sharpen, teach, prepare, or mature us? The reason caregivers can listen and exhibit presence is ultimately because of the belief that God can use all situations, especially painful ones, as part of the grand story of redemption and sanctification.

A final area of competence is essential: recognizing when to refer someone to those with more training. It's important not to "over-train" or prepare caregivers to work with complexities that go beyond their level. With additional pain and complexity come the need for care at higher levels of the triangle—care from those with greater expertise.

At the lowest level, caregivers should intentionally *not* be providing care for specific symptoms related to a person's psychological disorder. However, the idea isn't for a lay caregiver or church to refer them out and move on to the next person. The caregiver can say, "You are being 'treated' there, but you are being 'cared for' here." As someone gets higher-level care from a clinician, the goal is to also have a within-the-church presence to pray with them, share their joys and sorrows, and allow them to experience God's love in human form: "I am with you . . . even to the end of the age" (Matthew 28:20, NLT).

Supervise the Caregivers

The third task for the coordinator is the supervision of volunteers. Research indicates that in the clinical realm, the best predictor of therapeutic effectiveness is supervision. This is common knowledge among therapists: "Clinical supervision is the pinnacle of appropriate care, and without it, mental health professionals have difficulty in developing their knowledge, skills, and abilities."[3]

Supervision is especially important when delivering care through laypeople. Every leader we spoke with who had implemented this type of ministry recognized that some form of ongoing supervision is essential. Such a supervisory presence ensures accountability. It motivates creativity. It promotes ethical restraint. It maintains boundaries. It provides opportunities for ongoing training, asking questions ("How do you handle this type of issue?"), and refining skills. In short, supervision keeps caregivers on the high ground and prevents the well-intentioned volunteer from wandering into the "swamp."

One key skill for all coordinators is knowing when to pull in mental health specialists to guide the work of the ministry. Outside specialists can offer ongoing training to lay helpers or the congregation, answer questions, and even extend care to the caregivers if needed. One surveyed clinician offered the same top advice that we heard from many others: "Consult a mental health professional for guidance in program development and maintenance." On a similar note, another professional said, "Consult with those who are experienced so they can help establish a robust program. They can also help you know when to refer to outside services as needed."

Determine the Need and Connect People to Care

When a person in need makes the courageous choice to seek help, there should be someone who will understand that person's need, hold their hand, and funnel them to the right resources of the CARE triangle. That someone is the coordinator.

Remember Pastor Brent's discussion with Roni in chapter 1, and what would have happened if he already had a CARE strategy in his church? His next step would have been to have his volunteer coordinator call Roni. The coordinator would hear Roni's situation and probably have her fill out an intake form (such as the partial example shared in chapter 2) to capture the essential information.

Then the coordinator would think through what kind of care Roni needed. In that example, the coordinator might make at least three connections for Roni: a trained lay listener who could come alongside her quickly, a mental health professional, and specific resources in the community (such as a pregnancy center for her daughter).

Unique situations lead to different recommendations for care, as well as individualized efforts to create connection. For example, because Roni was caring for parents with dementia, what if the coordinator was aware of three or four other households in the church who had a similar situation? The coordinator might bring these families together and suggest that they support one another in a bimonthly small group. That would be an example of a high-impact addition to the church CARE strategy that would cost no money and yet would be life-giving and significant for the people involved.

The coordinator helps to fill out all levels of the triangle and connect people to it.

The Caregiver

The task of the caregiver is to sit close to the pain of others without getting burned or burned out. That can be difficult, and it requires someone who isn't just willing but able. While most Christians "care" on a theological or theoretical level, not all are able to be present with others while they're in pain. Here are two qualities needed to be a lay helper.

Simple Presence, Without the "Right" Words

The first quality a caregiver needs is to be comfortable with simply being a quiet, calming presence. People can often be self-condemning because they don't have the right words—the magic potion, the silver bullet, the precise intervention that will relieve pain, soothe, comfort, and make a horrible situation better. Yet listeners of all levels learn to be still, calm, and hopeful in the presence of other people's pain—and they don't feel compelled to fix things.

Not long ago, I (Jim) spoke with a new lay listener, a young mom named Rebecca, who shared these insights into what she was learning in her training:

> I realized that originally I was doing this all wrong. I got anxious, because I told myself that I had to say the right words. If I was competent, then I would know what to say and it would be helpful. But in reality, I *didn't* know what to say. So at first, I assumed that this just wasn't for me. Other people should do this work.

> But then I realized: I can sit with people. It helps to just listen when they want to talk. To go grocery shopping together and push the cart. To take a walk. Bake cookies. Visit others who are hurting. There's a lot I can do without saying anything and without knowing the right words.

Rebecca's confidence as a caregiver grew as she learned she wasn't responsible for having the perfect words to "make everything better."

Simple Compassion, Without "You Should" Declarations

The second quality a lay listener needs to develop is the ability to keep clear, unfiltered, ultra-certain viewpoints about how to solve a problem to themselves! It's easy to think the role of helper involves telling people what we think they should do . . . or what the Bible is telling them they should do . . . or what we would do if we were in their position and knew what we know about what the Bible says they should do. Yet those who "know" the right words to say and feel free to say them usually prove to be very unhelpful helpers. The point here is say *less*. Think about Job 2, and the mistakes of Job's friends. They knew the right thing to do, "for they saw that his suffering was too great for words" (Job 2:13, NLT). Then over dozens of interactions, they went ahead and burdened him with lots and lots of unhelpful words.

Caregivers and counselors are amused by Bob Newhart's classic "Stop It!" skit.[4] The humor derives from a therapist (Newhart's character) being both right and absolutely wrong. He is right in that the client must stop her fearful train of thought. But he is wrong in saying the solution is just to "Stop it!" If she could stop, she would. That she can't is why she needs the therapist in the first place! Or, in our example here, why she needs the church and the community.

Clearly, the advice of Job's friends and Newhart's character are ridiculously inadequate. They think they're offering profound advice, but their words are callous and simplistic.

Leading biblical counselor Paul David Tripp offers a different approach. He declares this profound truth: "I am deeply persuaded that the foundation for people-transforming ministry is not sound theology; it is love."[5] In other words, the key to effective care is not your perfect biblical thinking. It's a compassionate presence. It's a person grounded in God's Word through whom love, compassion, understanding, and presence is experienced. That a person be knowledgeable should be a given. But knowledge demonstrated through biblical competence must be experienced as loving companionship by the person in pain. Tripp reiterates the teaching of 1 Corinthians 13:1: Without love I would be a noisy gong or a clanging cymbal.

8

Listening

Learning the Power of Presence

Friendship . . . is the sort of love one can imagine between angels.

C. S. LEWIS, *The Four Loves*

One of the scariest moments of my (Shaunti's) life came with the words *breast cancer*. This medical journey was complex and intimidating, and I could feel myself constantly teetering on the edge of full-blown anxiety. What kept me sane was an invitation from my friend Sara, who lives across the street and has a firepit in her backyard. She suggested that I invite a few friends over each week just to be together. Sometimes I processed with them, and they handed me tissues when my fear leaked out as tears. Sometimes we would just sit and watch the fire crackle on a cold winter's night. It was their *presence* that mattered.

We often think that helping those in distress involves having the right words or the right advice that will "fix" the situation. Words can certainly be comforting. My friends had simple words of love and concern, and it also mattered to hear them say, "I'm so sorry." But we are wrong when we think it's primarily our words that will heal. They are secondary to the deeper healing agent of presence.

A caregiver who is good at the ministry of presence is someone who, as Romans 12:12 says, can be "patient in affliction" (NIV). To be patient is to not offer the "quick fix" or the "five steps to peace, happiness, and perpetual relief." Listening delivers a profound message to the one receiving care: *God is seeking our holiness, maturity, and devotion—even in times of suffering. Let's listen together to hear how God might bring about beauty amid this pain.* Listening takes us deep into conversation about what God might be doing.

So that you are aware of what will be asked of your lay volunteers, let's look at seven skills of great listening and patient presence.

Skill #1: Joining

We often view caring for others as something with a top-down flow. The "helper" delivers the needed resources, along with a special secret sauce. The one in need attends to the steps presented or instructed. It's the one in need who is expected to join the helper. This perspective, however, is not biblical—and it's not effective.

Instead, we're called to join someone in their need. To step into their world. To be present in their space, experience, and context. To deliberately set aside the option of being "above" them with the answers.

If you've ever seen the show *Undercover Boss*, you know the incredible, eye-opening understanding that comes when a powerful

CEO secretly sets aside the trappings of their role and spends a few days doing the job of someone who works multiple levels down the chain: the line cook in the restaurant or the package handler in the warehouse. As the CEO sits in the cafeteria, joining in the conversation with people who make the business run, a profound understanding often emerges. But it requires the CEO to deliberately connect with folks where they are.

In the same way, a caregiver who joins with someone in pain is able to truly "get" the other person. This type of joining is possible because, while each person's circumstances are unique, all of us know pain.

Skill #2: Broaching

Based on hundreds of years of maritime history, there's strict protocol for boarding a military vessel. If you're in uniform, you stop at the gangway and salute. If you're a civilian, you stand attentively. Then you say, "Request permission to come aboard." The salute is returned by the officer of the day, with permission granted or denied.

This protocol is as common as ringing a doorbell or knocking. You ask—you don't barge.

In the realm of caregiving, you're invited to ask. As a caregiver, you actually have the authority to ask. But you inquire with humility and respect. You don't assume, demand, or accuse. The phrase *broaching* is used to indicate that we ask to go places and pursue topics we wouldn't pursue unless we've joined and have been given permission. Caregivers must practice "requesting permission to come aboard": "It seems like you're sad. Would you like to talk?"

Two postures are essential for effective broaching: humility and observation.

The caregiver who exhibits humility in broaching suggests an openness and a willing spirit to walk close to the pain of another without needing to amplify it or minimize it. The message is, *I am willing to be with you, even in hard things.*

To broach effectively, we must also observe. One of our colleagues described being at a morning worship service at her church when she was also experiencing deep grief. She sang, prayed, and listened, like the others in the sanctuary. She thought her pain was invisible as she tried to hide in the anonymity of the balcony. But an acquaintance saw her. This woman approached and said something like "You seem distressed. Are you okay?" She invited our colleague to meet to talk and pray.

Look at the power of this action. She didn't wait. She initiated. But she did so by invitation only. She was given permission to "come aboard."

Skill #3: Being a Soothing Presence

The psalmist shares a crucial source of joy, pivoting on an essential word. He writes, "You make known to me the path of life; in your *presence* there is fullness of joy; at your right hand are pleasures forevermore" (Psalm 16:11, emphasis added).

The path is made known through the experience of *presence*. Presence is soothing—or at least it can be, if it's done correctly. Some types of soothing presence might surprise you. We tend to think of it as sitting near another person and saying nice things. For example, if someone is in grief, we assume that encouraging them to just "talk it out" is always healing and restorative. The mental picture is of talking quietly on a couch, hankie in hand. And that picture does ring true for many people.

But for many others, regardless of their issue, a soothing presence involves activity. In particular, activities with repetitive motion and/or no complex thinking tend to be helpful to the overstretched brain. Playing pickleball. Going to a movie. Raking leaves. Talking requires effort to think of the words to be said, but in many cases, especially when someone is sad, all the words have been chased out of their mind. Doing something where the person doesn't have to make conversation or decisions can be more powerful than exchanging words. It's not just the activity but the activity with another that amplifies healing.[1]

Side-by-side activity is especially important for some boys and men, whose brains may feel that sense of "fight, flight, or freeze" when someone looks directly in their eyes and asks about their feelings. They may find it easier to open up when driving in the car side by side or when doing an activity together.

For some, the activity of *making* something is particularly restorative. Baking a cake. Painting a picture. Building that long-needed border around the herb garden.

Laypeople should consider all these options when they connect with someone. Recent research indicates that healing is enhanced by activity.[2]

I (Jim) have experienced this personally. When my father died at ninety-three years old, I was grieving. I needed to mourn. But I wasn't sure how. His house needed to be cleaned out and painted, but I had lectures to prepare. So as I was painting his living room, I was listening to a podcast about limbic brain activity. (Yes, you can laugh at me!) As I was rolling on the paint, I heard a renowned psychologist explain that the most productive recovery of grief, especially for males, is to go make something better. Build a table. Fix a leak. Run in a race. Then he added, "And it is best that you do this with a friend." I realized that, by accident, I was doing "sort of good." In my grief recovery, I was being active and making something better. But I was doing it alone. My recovery was delayed because I was void of others who could grieve with me.

Skill #4: Grounding

When a house is struck by lightning, it absorbs all the energy. The result is that every unprotected electronic appliance is fried through the electrical surge. By contrast, tall buildings typically have some type of "grounding"—a system that diverts the electricity to the ground.

Pain is like lightning. It can absorb all our energy. It can be all we think about from the moment we rise until we return to rest—and fry our hearts, minds, and relationships.

In the realm of people care, grounding refers to changing our focus and diverting our attention, the way a grounding wire diverts electricity. While the brain wants to focus on everything related to pain, it is possible to redirect the brain's attention. This is something a layperson can train someone to do.

One way to do this is by using the senses to be aware of what's around us. Take a moment to look around you. What do you see? Notice everything and say it. Now pause. What do you hear? Identify the sounds: children playing outside, the rhythmic sound of the dishwasher, the furnace or fan circulating air. What do you smell? The fish from last night's dinner. The fragrance of fabric softener clinging to your clothes. What do you feel? Literally, what is touching your skin? Feel the shoes that encase your feet. The table your arms are resting on. Now feel inside. Note the tension in the abdomen. The moisture in your mouth.

Grounding is far more than a diversionary tactic. It calms the brain and prepares it for an action other than pain management. Doing this exercise helps turn on your brain's creativity switch and funnel you into a different way of thinking. Caregivers assist in locating mature, hopeful, and healing grounding experiences.

Grounding is similar to the meditative experience some may feel when they walk into a hushed church before a worship service or into a prayer meeting that's about to start. We sit quietly in preparation to encounter God, placing our minds at rest so we can listen, praise, and learn. Grounding creates space for the brain to think, create, and solve.

Skill #5: Reflecting Content and Emotion

Outside the counseling realm, people often minimize the benefits of reflecting, or mirroring what someone is saying back to them. To reflect is to return an idea or a thought to the one who first spoke. When you tell someone in pain, "It sounds like all that time in the hospital was exhausting," it says, "I get you. I see you. I understand you." When you reflect, you're not trying to be original, cute, flashy, funny, or engaging. You're trying to say, "You are heard."

Lay caregivers learn how to reflect content (what happened) *and* emotion (the meaning attached to it). For example, "I heard you say that you've never felt so discouraged and alone as the day your spouse deployed overseas and that you have no idea what you're going to do." We can teach people to say what they hear, not what they've felt in similar situations or what they think someone *should* feel. Holding up the mirror in this way invites the person to both feel understood and examine themselves. If the person is thinking about things in a distorted way ("Is it true that I've never felt this alone? What are a few things I actually could do?"), this practice invites them to alter how they see the situation.

Skill #6: Clarifying

At times, it's good to be wrong. Clarifying involves asking questions that help bring dysregulated or confused speech into focus. For example, "I heard you say that the day was so discouraging. That you felt lost, confused, and afraid. Of those three, which would you like to talk about?"

Our pain is usually not expressed with clear-thinking logic. Sometimes it's delivered with tears and a runny nose. Sometimes the words are suppressed and don't flow with clarity. And sometimes the words are exaggerated or even mean.

Frequently, the listener doesn't even understand the words, because the speaker isn't making sense. Pain usually has bad grammar and punctuation! Emotionally laden language tends to ramble, be disjointed, or be interrupted by weeping. So it's easy for a listener to be confused or lose track.

To clarify is to ask, "Did I hear you right when you said [fill in the blank]?" When the answer to that question is "No, not really," the person is prompted to dig a little deeper to explain what they actually think—something they might not have done to this extent before. Or when the answer to that question is "Oh . . . I didn't realize my words sounded so harsh," the person may be prompted to recognize how they sound to their loved ones during a hard time.

Skill #7: Summarizing

In the context of listening, summarizing is when we boil down what someone is saying into a single idea. Doing so suggests progress and offers validation. For example, "You have expressed yourself so clearly today. Thank you for sharing. We covered a lot. I heard you say that . . ."

Not only is summarizing essential for the one seeking care; it's also essential for the caregiver. It creates a structure to end a conversation. We've all been in uncomfortable situations when a person's pain is so great that their words only have an accelerator and no brake. Summarizing helps the caregiver bring the conversation to a close in a way that's beneficial for both the listener and the person sharing.

Setting You Up for Success

Pastors who understand the value of presence can preach it, model it, pursue potential helpers who offer it, and emphasize training that supports it. The points in this chapter just scratch the surface. We offer more in-depth manuals, videos, and instructions at Thechurchcares.com. Other ministries such as Stephen Ministries and the American Association of Christian Counseling's Mental Health Coach certification offer free or tuition-based training in fundamental listening skills.

As your caregivers learn these technical listening skills, they will also need your encouragement to lean in to a crucial nontechnical one: listening to the voice of One who cares far more than any caregiver ever will. As one women's ministry director emphasized, "We have seen the vast importance of prayer in our church's caregiver roles. We have no life-changing power until we ourselves are 'plugged in' and asking God for His wisdom and His words. He has helped me see over and over again what I never would have seen on my own!"

9

Managing Emotions

Helping Feelings Be a Teacher, Not a Tyrant

Between stimulus and response there is a space. In that space is our power to choose our response. In our response lies our growth and our freedom.

VIKTOR E. FRANKL

Dogs and cats. Birds and fish. We call them pets. We love them, and they love us. (Except maybe fish. They don't care about us, but they look cool!) They're a source of comfort, joy, entertainment, and support. They encourage, soothe, and reassure. But in the animal kingdom, the lists of dogs, cats, birds, and fish include wolves, lions, raptors, and piranhas. These are not pets but predators. They don't entertain us. They eat us.

We tend to view emotions the way we view animals. We view "good" emotions like cherished pets; they bring out the best in life. And we see "bad" emotions as predators that can make us their noon meal. Good emotions are welcomed—sometimes obsessively pursued. Painful emotions are avoided, suppressed, and denied.

The Christian tradition and the Bible offer a very different perspective. All emotions are intended to teach us. In his book *Sacred Marriage*, Gary Thomas proposes a question that is useful for everyone to consider—children, adolescents, and adults, whether married or single: the question of whether God is more interested in our holiness than our happiness.[1] In other words, what if emotions such as happiness are not the main goal in life?

Now, just to be clear, Gary is *not* saying people shouldn't want to be happy, and neither are we. In response to that common misunderstanding, Gary says, "We should absolutely hope for a happy, abundant life and marriage. That is God's best intention for us! But we also have to see everything in life that stretches us as a means of growing us."[2]

All emotions—the joyful and the painful—are meant to shape us into who God created us to be. To teach us to persevere. To make us holy.

It's essential for caregivers to know about emotions (their own and others')—how useful they can be for healing and how, when mishandled, they can lead to ineffective care. The three emotions that are most commonly labeled as negative are anger, sadness, and fear.

If lay caregivers aren't prepared to address these intense emotions, they won't be fruitful or productive, and they may be tempted to quit prematurely. But if they *are* prepared to address them, dramatic healing can take place.

Seven Skills for Handling Intense Emotions

To be effective at offering care, a caregiver must develop skills that help them respond wisely to intense emotions. The following list includes skills that pastors and coordinators, as executives and managers, must make sure the team develops. It also represents a start for leaders to evaluate how prepared a potential volunteer is to address the needs of others. If you believe someone already has these foundations, they may be a good candidate.

Skill #1: Learning from Our Experience with Anger, Sadness, and Fear

It's often said that "wounded healers make the best healers." Although there are exceptions, that's true of most people who become caregivers. Many lay counselors (and psychologists, counselors, and pastors) are motivated to care for others in part by their own suffering—painful emotions, trauma, and personal crises. Their philosophy is "I want to give back," reflecting the virtues of 2 Corinthians 1:3-4. Not only do they want to help, but they want to do it *well.*

Counseling scholar Tristram Jones focused his research on "wounded healers." He identified many reasons wounded healers are good helpers, saying, "Many writers have detailed the contributions of counselors who enter the field armed with the special insights born of personal recovery." He describes eight ways our previous pain facilitates effectiveness in caring for others.[3] It offers:

- insight into others
- increased identification with those suffering
- contagious zeal for healing
- decreased judgment and condescension
- inspiring hope

- ability to be direct
- capacity to be a role model
- authority to describe the long journey ahead

These are all benefits a lay caregiver (or any caregiver!) can embrace.

Skill #2: Learning to Lose Our Experience of Anger, Sadness, and Fear

However, it's not enough to have walked through suffering firsthand. The pain that helpers have experienced can also create an obstacle to care if they aren't prepared. According to Jones, the most substantial barrier is the propensity for their own anger, sadness, or fear to come back.[4] Additional concerns include blurred boundaries (for example, if a caregiver learns something that might impact a mutual friend), a tendency to read their own experience into the lives of others, and an assumption that the other person is in denial when they don't identify with the life experience of the caregiver.

Or, if the caregiver has been depressed, they have some estimation of the discouragement of others. "Some estimation" is the operating phrase, and it must stop there. The listener needs to set themselves aside to some degree and take on a sense of humility and curiosity about the other person.

Skill #3: Learning to Read Emotions Like Farmers Read Soil

My (Shaunti's) husband, Jeff, grew up in a farming community, living not far from the family farms where both his parents were born and lived. If you ask any farmer, having abundant crops depends on having good, deep, nitrogen-rich soil. Farmers work with what's growing and visible, but they can't attend to *only* what they can see. It's the same with caregivers. We can get stuck on the surface emotions and lose sight of the source.

Reading the soil allows us to uncover and discuss what's underneath—such as the beliefs that drive the feelings. Anger might follow perceived injustice. Depression is often a response to powerlessness. Anxiety is usually a belief in future harm. The caregiver can see that the real concerns to talk about—injustice, powerlessness, and harm—are hidden by the emotion. They recognize that if they only attend to the emotion, they might not get to the actual concern.

Once the source is addressed, much can be understood—by both the helper and the help seeker. For example, a wife might feel upset and uncared for because her husband has become angry and withdrawn. In many cases, neither party recognizes anger for what it is: a sign of emotional pain in the relationship. Perhaps, for instance, he feels the sting of frequent criticism. She can explain what she's feeling and why, but he may not be able to. Both of them may feel that his anger is wrong or uncalled for. So he locks down. And she experiences her own anger at his withdrawal.

When a caregiver helps both people see that their anger is a signal of pain (just as crying would be), they can discuss the real issues that matter to each of them and that both can address.

Because someone's anger usually makes us uncomfortable, it's easy to view it as uncaring or just wrong. But although the Bible says, "In your anger do not sin" (Ephesians 4:26, NIV), anger itself is not a sin. The issue is what we do with that emotion. Anger—or any other emotion—becomes sinful when we use it to manipulate, dominate, retaliate against, or abuse someone else (or even ourselves).

In order to stay close to someone in pain, caregivers must recognize their own reactions when they get close to someone else's intense emotions. For example, a listener might realize: "I get confused." "I argue back." "I want to say, 'Hey, if you don't want my help, *fine*!'" "I feel sad myself." "I get so nervous—then I ruminate for days about what I said and didn't say and why I did it so poorly!"

With insight and awareness, the caregiver can discover a greater sense of calm in the presence of others' intensity. That calmness has a healing quality in itself. We're drawn to those who aren't rattled when there's turmoil. Think of Jesus sleeping in the boat before He calmed the sea. That's the kind of presence that will grow in your lay helpers as they walk in this ministry.

We suspect you can see the value of having some of these folks in your church.

Skill #4: Learning to See Purpose in Anger, Sadness, and Fear

All emotions have a purpose. In fact, they are *created by God* for a purpose. Because it can be uncomfortable to sit with someone in distress, caregivers often find it transformative to see God's purpose in negative emotions and, over time, help the other person see that purpose too.

James had a great perspective: "Let *perseverance* finish its work so that you may be mature and complete, not lacking anything" (James 1:4, NIV, emphasis added). Perseverance is what enables us to hang on through difficult circumstances. The reason we need to persevere through our trials (and as we care for others in theirs) is because they're often full of pain! These feelings bring us to our knees—one way or another.

A painful season is a school. And with the ministry and perspective of the church, it can be a school where the person learns to see God at work. To trust Him. To learn biblical and psychological techniques for persevering and managing emotions. Any emotion that might lead us into a downward spiral must be managed, lest it control us.

As we learn to manage our emotions, the benefits can be profound. In the research for my (Shaunti's) book *The Surprising Secrets of Highly Happy Marriages*, one of the habits of the healthiest and happiest couples was that they "bossed their feelings around," rather than letting their feelings boss them around. That phrase came from a wife who described this realization: "[I need] to remind myself to keep what I'm believing [and feeling] in check. My self-talk has power, and I need to boss it around a bit."[5]

Skill #5: Learning to Check the Gauges for Accuracy

Sometimes our emotional gauges are broken. Helpers are often called to sit with people who are sad, fearful, or frustrated—for no quantifiable reason. These people don't want to feel sad, but they do. They want to turn over all their pain to Jesus and live free from the weight of their pain. But they can't. They've searched high and low for unconfessed sin, for the impact of trauma, and for the consequences of poor choices, but they find no cause. There's no causal sin. No childhood abuse or mistreatment. They're just . . . sad.

Caregivers learn that some people are more prone to emotional reactivity and there's no specific cause. Some people's brains experience a higher or lower intensity of emotions, in much the same way that some brains are more or less artistic, or more or less capable of spatial recognition or remembering names or numbers. But where too much (or too little) emotional reactivity is getting in the way of handling life well, caregivers can play an essential role in guiding people toward medical intervention when needed.

People with intense reactions can feel guilty because of these emotions. In the Christian community, some people may think that such feelings indicate a lack of faith or a failure to turn a problem over to God. That means discouragement, fear, or anger produce guilt on top of the preexisting feelings!

Now, remember, sometimes intense emotions are crucial life indicators, so we need to trust them. But they can over- or under-describe reality. Therefore, it is good to have others help discern them. And sometimes they are misleading and dangerous. There, physicians can offer guidance toward medications to restore the brain's ability to send accurate emotional messages. When the "gauges" are broken, the right medical attention is often a relief.

In my current research for a book project about what helps individuals with their own mental health, I (Shaunti) can't count the number of people who used a word picture like this one, from a woman with bipolar disorder and other serious mental illness:

> Not having medication when you need it is like getting up in the morning and leaving the house—but forgetting your glasses. Everything is blurred and foggy. You can still see, but it's unclear. Taking your meds and doing these things to

focus yourself is like putting on glasses. The fog may still be there, but it isn't weighing on you.

One pastor told us, "I'm troubled by how many people take medication to manage symptoms without pursuing the root causes of those symptoms. Yet it's also true that if I'm someone in a hard place and my issues are debilitating and keeping me from functioning, medication can help me become functional enough that I can begin to ask questions about what's going on underneath and find real healing."

Skill #6: Learning to Handle Hot Emotions

Intense emotion from others often prompts withdrawal. Hot emotions make us hot, so we want to hose them down instead of allowing them to help us learn.

Think about how you feel when you're in front of a dog that's growling and baring its teeth. We certainly don't extend a caring hand—we back away! Anger has the same effect. So does extreme sadness and heightened fear. Our instinct is to back away.

With these "hot" emotions, a caregiver may naturally want to calm the person down. That impulse is usually for the sake of the listener, not the one in need. The logic is "You're upset, and I'm here to help. Please calm down so I can help you."

If this is our response, we are probably—without intending to be—enrolled in the "friends of Job" school of care (Job 42:7-9).

The lesson good caregivers learn is to remain calm when things are hot. To stay relaxed when the other person isn't. It's essential to practice doing something that doesn't come naturally: remaining in the presence of someone who is experiencing hot emotions.

In situations like this, it helps to go back to the analogy about reading the soil. For example, instead of thinking about the anger we see (which can be intimidating), we can think about the experience of injustice underneath it. Anger exists in the absence of fairness and justice. We may want to avoid anger or rage, but we can approach and enter into a concern about injustice. It's easier to sit with someone talking about perceived unfairness than it is to sit with someone who feels rage.

Or consider great sadness. A grief has occurred that someone feels powerless to change. Something we expected to always be there has been lost and, with it, the hope of recovery. Talking about hopelessness can feel like a black hole—there are no sides and no end. But we can talk about and empathize with deeply felt unmet expectations.

Or consider fear. It's anticipatory. It's ahead, not behind. The horizon carries danger as one moves toward it. Anxiety is worry about what might happen—something that could result in calamity or great pain. We want to flee fear, but we can approach and engage with uncertainty about the future.

In understanding these three emotions, a caregiver can ask about the stories behind them. Hearing the stories allows a caregiver to approach, not flee.

Skill #7: Learning to Use an Old Tool for a New Purpose

Reinhold Niebuhr crafted a powerful and useful prayer that many people know as the Serenity Prayer:

God, grant me the serenity to accept the things I cannot change,
the courage to change the things I can,
and the wisdom to know the difference.[6]

This prayer captures many aspects of showing care to someone, but it's especially relevant when it comes to helpers who are learning to be present with intense emotions and aid those who experience them. The layperson knows that while emotions may be painful, they aren't the enemy but the indicator—like a warning indicator on the car dashboard.

Emotions can prompt us to act. In the world of psychology, we call this self-efficacy. That's another way of saying that the person can do something about the way they're feeling. When we act, the emotion decreases. The warning light shuts off after we put air in the tires.

Unfortunately, a person sometimes has intense emotions but can't undo the damage or the outcome. Imagine that Marc never smoked a day in his life but just learned he has lung cancer because of his genetics. It can't be fixed, it can't be undone, and it wasn't his fault. He experiences all three emotions: intense anger because he has a life-threatening illness, the discouragement of knowing that treatment will be long and costly, and fear about the future for his wife and kids.

Some emotions arise from unchangeable and no-fault facts. Those are situations the person must come to accept, hopefully with our help. We can approach this intense pain much like we would approach a memorial to tragedy such as the 9/11 Memorial, the Holocaust Memorial Museum, or the Tomb of the Unknown Soldier. We stand with others, unable to alter the past or bring back the fallen. We do not eliminate the suffering; we help the person create courage in the midst of it. It's in this that healing comes.

We can step into this space with the Serenity Prayer. Marc's intense, emotion-laden reality can't be changed—but his attitude and trust in God can. This is where the caregiver can come alongside the person in pain to help them hear from the Lord: "My grace is sufficient for you" (2 Corinthians 12:9).

Emotions aren't something to avoid. They're created by God to be our companions. They guide us, help us prioritize what's important, and prevent us from making poor decisions. This is true both for those emotions that we keep as pets and for those that run in packs in the forest. Churches must prepare caregivers to sit with the intensity and not be consumed by it. To remain close to the center of the flame and not be burned. By learning to offer a calm presence amid emotional storms, the layperson's help goes beyond the person in need. Such a presence helps enrich the whole church community.

10

Healing Relationships

Being Present in the Space Between People

Be united with other Christians. A wall with loose bricks is not good. The bricks must be cemented together.

CORRIE TEN BOOM

Relationships are one of the main sources of mental health distress. Conflict between a husband and a wife. Between a parent and a child. Between a bully and a target.

Lay caregivers learn that the work of care is often not focused on people. It's focused on the space between people.

At times, the conflicted space between people is insulated or distancing, like a wall. Other times the space is a battleground, where harsh words are shot at the other person in an effort to cause harm or to gain control.

Conflict emerges between a wife and a husband as they share a home, children, finances, a bed, a car—even a closet. Conflict resides in the space between parents and adolescents as parents seek to provide, oversee, and promote the well-being of their family, while the emerging adult exercises their wings and tries to fly. (Sometimes they launch before they're capable of sustained flight—and sometimes they remain in the nest long after they can fly.) It's the space between adults and their elderly parents as the responsibility for care gradually shifts from the older to the younger generation. And it's the tension between church members with different views about marriage, baptism, or how to handle the pastor search.

These relational conflicts start within us—something disturbs our priorities or expectations about how things should work—and then they leak into the space between us and the other person. James refers to this reality when he asks, "What causes fights and quarrels among you? Don't they come from your desires that battle within you?" (James 4:1, NIV).

Christian peacemakers need to step into these spaces—and in doing so, they can help bring a great deal of healing to many lives and to the church itself.

The Uniqueness of Relationship Work

We will cover the skills needed to step into this work shortly. But because caring for relationship needs can be both a vitally important and a unique process, there are a few big-picture points for every leader to keep in mind first.

Relationship Work Looks Below the Surface

When there's relational conflict, we see the evidence externally: the emotion is expressed through volume, distancing, or power—or all three. So it's tempting to focus our attention on the outside evidence of the conflict, such as yelling or sarcasm. And the behavior may, in fact, need to be addressed. However, if that's all we do, we may feel better temporarily because the space between us has been addressed for the moment. But the internal conflict, the battle within (the confusion, hurt, or unhappiness due to unmet expectations) remains.

When churches help the parties look below the surface, they provide an environment where relationships can thrive—but this is inevitably a messy process. Where there's growth, tension may also be present. Ideally, the caregiver's job is to help the reverse be true as well: to bring individual and group growth out of the conflict—for example, by helping those in conflict learn to set and honor boundaries.

The care leadership team will create that type of direction and policy, and find and train those who are led to work with relationships—and have the temperament to do so.

Relationship Work Can Be Both Complex *and* Present Lay Care Opportunities

Simple and effective lay care relationship efforts may frequently support the work of a therapist.

Relationship work is often more complex simply because caregivers may be sitting with two or more people (such as spouses, friends, parents, children, or colleagues) who are experiencing relational tension, insecurity, and frustration. Their role is to encourage and support. They will not be intervening as a clinician would. Also, it's rare for lay caregivers to sit with entire families who are in conflict. That's something therapists, psychologists, or counselors are trained to do, and because there are often many layers to these issues, we recommend seeking someone with training and experience in such cases.

But all that said, within the lay care space, there is much that can be done to help relationships. For example, it's very common for couples and families to need good models to follow—such as examples found in church friendships—to support their relationships in general or their work in therapy.

A while back, I (Jim) was meeting with a couple who frequently bickered and argued. I asked about their social support, and the husband said, "Well, actually, our marriage is better than all of our friends'. We fight, but we haven't been unfaithful. We don't get drunk and yell at each other. We are never physically threatening. Yeah, we're bad . . . but our friends are awful! We don't know anyone who has a good marriage."

Trying not to show my *Well, that explains a lot* feeling on my face, I responded, "I have a suggestion. I would like you to contact your pastor and ask him to assign a mentoring couple to you. A couple with a healthy marriage. You are to have dinner. Hang out. Visit their home. Watch, ask, and listen as to how they do marriage."

This type of intervention is ridiculously simple—and effective. In many cases, good marriages can offer an influence beyond anything provided by a therapist.

In fact, marriage and family mentoring is one of the most effective strategies in creating stability for the whole family. It's common for struggling couples to talk with mentor couples about how to be successful in their marriage journey. It's also common for parents to seek wisdom and guidance from the church community about giving their kids the best chance to thrive. Adult children often seek the support of the church and caregivers to ease the physical and emotional burden of caring for an ailing parent.

Relationship Work Requires a "Switzerland" Temperament

To work with people on relationships, the caregiver will be very close to the pain of others (the "fights and quarrels" referenced in James 4). So how do they do that? You will see seven key skills below. But there's one that matters above others. I (Jim) speak from thirty years of experience sitting with thousands of conflicted couples and families and having learned from countless mistakes when I say this. And I'm emphasizing this because it's really that important!

> *Pastors, one of your most difficult yet most essential responsibilities is to prepare lay caregivers not to be judge or referee with those in conflict. At this lay level of care, they should not be placing themselves between the conflicted couple. The skill they need to learn is to remain present and offer validity to each person.*

As we'll discuss shortly, people in conflict try to pull the caregiver toward their side of the fray—to make it "me and you" against "that other person." If they succeed, the result is a decrease in the visible battle and an increase in the war within. The conflict will live to fight another day—and will likely be louder and more severe next time. So just as with geopolitical conflict, the caregiver must be "Switzerland"—an engaged third party whom everyone can trust to not take sides. And whom everyone can trust to establish clear processes, maintain safety, and be the "adult in the room" when emotions are running high. (We should clarify that every church will probably encounter couples who *do* need a referee—someone to control the space and stop a cycle of injury. That type of couple intervention is a "step up" from lay caregiving. When a couple lacks the ability to regulate emotions and is prone to conduct that has negative consequences, pastors and coordinators should remain watchful to ensure that those couples receive the appropriate higher level of care.)

The biblical text, Christian tradition, and psychological research all offer ideas and direction for how to sit in the presence of others when addressing relational, marital, and family concerns. Following are seven skills for pastors and coordinators to teach lay caregivers sitting with people in relational tension. We offer a few techniques, but as you can probably guess, the techniques aren't what people need most. Rather, it's spiritual disciplines such as patience and self-control that allow the caregiver to remain present and close while others are tense and emotionally elevated.

Seven Skills for Relational Caregiving

These skills are starting points. We share them not so that someone can absorb them and immediately provide care but so that you as the pastor can understand what is needed in potential volunteers and what will be taught and overseen by the coordinator. Detailed resources (including videos, manuals, and documents) are available through The Church Cares website.

Skill #1: Offering a Calming Presence

The tagline for a successful television marketing campaign was "Never let them see you sweat." We're not advocating an antiperspirant brand or implying that the caregiver will be unencumbered by concern. What we're saying is that in relational caregiving, calmness wins.

People seek care when they're emotionally dysregulated—in other words, when they're having trouble managing their feelings. So it can be a powerful part of the healing process to have a caregiver who is emotionally engaged in the story but not given over to controlling emotions like fear or resentment. The first task for any caregiver, no matter the concern, is to embody these words of Jesus in John 14:27: "Peace I leave with you; my peace I give to you. Not as the world gives do I give to you. Let not your hearts be troubled, neither let them be afraid."

We can retain and convey a genuine calming presence when we grasp the truth that "fixing the problem" isn't up to us, but up to God. It also helps to grasp that our task is to remain close to each person—even if they resist every idea we offer. Such responses embody grace. Megan Fate Marshman wrote a useful book on how to remain in a place of rest under any circumstances. She notes that Jesus displayed a consistent trait in all His dealings: He was relaxed.[1] In the clinical world we call this a "non-anxious presence." A presence like this is contagious.

It's also something we must (ironically) fight for. When people are upset, they often do things that spur those around them to be upset with them. There's a subconscious (and mistaken) assumption that they'll feel better when other people are as upset as they are! Caregivers learn to recognize the pull to join the negativity and instead serve empathy and calm understanding. This is an exhibition of leadership. A non-anxious presence declares, "Follow me; I will lead you out of this swamp."

Many parents understand this concept instinctively. When a storm is bearing down, the power is off, and the children are frightened, parents don't openly enter into the fear. Instead, they are courageous and reassuring—even if it's an act. But that act helps the confidence become real, for the child *and* for the parents.

Have you ever watched an unflappable gate agent at the airport as they manage dozens of people who are upset about a canceled flight? It's magic. It's music. The best agents offer empathy and support in the midst of a frustrating reality no one can fix. No matter the emotional intensity, they are diligent in their task. They don't engage in shouting matches or heated conversations regarding factors out of their control.

Pastors model, practice, and teach this kind of non-anxious presence every day in a stunning number of tense, complex situations that would send many other people into a tailspin. Caregivers are to mimic this same quality.

Just as the airline ticket agent is trained, caregivers must rehearse and develop this skill. One example is to ask student caregivers, "Recall a time when you were in a leadership role but lost your emotional regulation. What got to you?" And "Now think of how you would talk yourself through a different emotional response to the same situation. Let's practice it." We want the caregiver to imagine themselves being close to someone who is upset—not trying to minimize their pain but remaining close to them in their agitation.

Skill #2: Dealing with Triangulation

When there is tension in relationships, people can try to get their way by manipulating or leveraging others to take their side. Triangulation occurs when your friends or family members are not getting along with each other and when each of them does their best to pressure you to join forces with them against the other person. You feel the pull in the form of guilt and "How could you?" or "I thought you were my friend." The relational tug is actually triangulation, and it exists when there's relational tension.

Learning how to recognize and respond to this pull is one of the more advanced skills we mentioned—as are several others you'll see below. Yet because these methods have so many applications, lay caregivers, marriage mentors, and small group leaders may also want access to these tools.

Here's the key: overcoming triangulation is *only* possible if you don't allow yourself to be the referee. If you find yourself saying one-sided things like "Well, you know, Noah, she makes a good point. I can see why that hurt her," you've already lost. Remember, the goal isn't to figure out who is right. The goal is to restore the relationship. (And if a lay caregiver starts feeling like they want to take sides with a particular spouse, it's probably the type of complex situation that should be escalated to a professional therapist.)

As mentioned, it's common for a caregiver to feel like both parties are manipulating their emotions or causing them to feel like a traitor. That's why training is so important: it prepares a caregiver to remain steady when they feel yanked in different directions.

The essence of this skill is to connect with one person, then connect with the other—in the presence of both!—and to legitimize the concerns of all involved without getting consumed by them. The message conveyed is the same message a parent conveys when mediating between warring children: "I care for both of you. If I can connect with both of you, if I can see both sides, then so can each of you—together."

This skill is taught by observation and rehearsal. The most effective learning experience for the caregiver is to observe this vortex of emotional tug-of-war firsthand so they can see how it's handled—and learn that they, too, can (with training and practice) handle it. It's also immensely helpful to hear other caregivers process their own personal responses to triangulation (perhaps during supervision times, in ways that are consistent with the church's confidentiality guidelines). Caregivers learn by recreating the pull between two parties and rehearsing responses that do not take sides.

For example, a caregiver speaking with a father (Nathan) and his adolescent son (Jayden) might say, "Jayden, I hear your father's worry for your safety and that he doesn't want you dead from Saturday night crazies on the road. And Nathan, I hear from your son that he is aware of his responsibilities with the car, even though he did let things get out of hand last week with the speeding ticket." Then the caregiver might say to both, "I see you two needing to figure out a path for Jayden to learn how to be an adult, while you parents can be reassured that he will not get killed in the process. I think you both want the same thing: for Jayden to grow up and not be irresponsible about it. Jayden, you have to help your dad let go of his son. And Nathan, you have to help your son be an emerging adult. Both of you have to make the other person successful."

Skill #3: Moving from Blame to Contrition and Collaboration

With most issues affecting relationships, *each person* has played some part in creating the concern and *each person* carries some role in creating the resolution. Yet most people don't recognize that at the outset. Rather, they tend to see and express (sometimes with volume!) the specific things the other party has done to create the problem and their exact failure in not fixing it. While this may be our natural inclination, blame, scapegoating, and denial seldom promote healing. Instead, they're usually followed by some form of retaliation.

To overcome this type of stalemate, the caregiver can encourage each person to express contrition and pursue repair, even when they're hurt or upset. For example, suppose a feud between two local ministry directors has broken out, and they need help reconciling so they can work together again. Rather than ruminating on the other person's violation, both are prompted by the caregiver to finish this sentence: "I think a problem I can tackle is [fill in the blank]. Would that be helpful?"

To rebuild the relationship, each might be prompted to sincerely finish this sentence: "While the problem is mine and not yours, I could use your help in this way: [fill in the blank]." Both of those prompts might result in one party saying something like this: "I think I overreact. Could you let me know when you feel that I'm overreacting?"

In learning sessions, caregivers practice statements like these. They create scenarios, imagining how a party might seek to "blow up the conversation" and then offering responses to keep everyone on track.

Caregivers must learn how to take control of the conversation at those pivotal moments. This is where the primary tool of a listening presence gives way to action. When blame is blowing up the conversation, that is the time not to passively listen but to step in, protect, and invite—on both sides. Contrition met with contrition produces reconciliation. But if it's met with blame, rejection, or disregard, the conflict will escalate.

Caregivers bring people to the point of contrition through their calming presence and mutual validation. Contrition isn't where the conversation starts. But it's where you aim to end after engaging each person.

Skill #4: Honoring Both Individuality and Connection

There's a conundrum that every culture, clan, family, and marriage must address, an enigma that has existed since the Garden. It has to do with being singular and plural at the same time. Each person is both a "me" and a "we." For every human, being an individual and being in community are in constant tension.

Every person—and every group—negotiates the tension between "me" and "we" through an exchange of privileges and obligations—there's a reciprocating cycle of giving and receiving. For example, when an eighth-grade boy stays home to watch his younger siblings while his parents go out for a date night, he fulfills an obligation or a duty to his family group. But he may carry a bit of resentment for being the only one of his friends to stay home and miss the basketball game. When you're fourteen, that's a big "give." Yet on another occasion, his parents are up most of the night hosting the eighth-grade graduation pool party. While no self-respecting middle schooler would acknowledge this form of giving and receiving—his duty to his parents and the duty his parents have to him—he knows it, he sees it, and he feels it. It's fair.

While we all know that life isn't fair in the sense of perfect balance, we also know that when we give to the group and when the group honors and promotes us as an individual, it allows for healthy, secure relationships.

Here's the issue: it's common for caregivers to hear about what *hasn't* felt fair in someone's marriage, family, or group. In every cluster of people, there are fault lines of unfairness that threaten to shake the earth and cause the structure to collapse. Yet caregivers *cannot* create fairness. They don't rebuild family boundaries, for example. They can't make sure the giving and receiving between every member is balanced and mutually gratifying.

But they can and should ask, "When it doesn't feel fair, what do *you* do?" That question and the inquiries that follow promote greater balance in the giving and receiving that happens in a relationship. The goal of these conversations is to bring honor to the "me" *and* the "we."

Skill #5: Thinking in Levels, Not in Lines

The classic game of tic-tac-toe is a linear game. Three figures in a straight line, and you win!

Relationships, however, don't follow lines. They're dimensional—they exist on multiple levels. People are spouses, parents, siblings, workers, students, and neighbors, with each role requiring a unique language and set of expectations. Which means relational care is also like a "whack a mole" game. You make a hit here . . . and it pops up again over there!

As a result of these dimensions, when people are in conflict, they tend to be in different planes of reality—which is why so many arguments get stuck. Each person is working toward a different goal. And each is arguing about different things!

For example, imagine if a married couple had an argument about a burned breakfast that ended up spiraling into two days of silence. You can think of what they're arguing about existing on three levels at once.

First, there's the *topic* of tension. In this case, the toast got burned and breakfast was ruined. If they both agree that burned toast and a ruined breakfast is bad, and that's all there is to it, then there is no argument.

Often, though, one is on the level of toast while the other is at a second and deeper level: the *pattern* of tension. For example, perhaps this isn't an isolated incident. Perhaps the disappointment from elevated hope and lost expectations has occurred many times before—and in areas far more important than breakfast. Thus, one person feels on edge, almost expecting that something will happen to disappoint them. So when the breakfast is burned, they end up saying something big that may seem out of proportion to the other party. Like "I can never trust you to do something as simple as making breakfast." The spiral accelerates rapidly.

The final level they may be arguing about is the *reminder* of tension. Everyone has a lifetime of coping with failures and disappointments. For this couple, who is now on a hair trigger for problems, this ruined breakfast and the other person's reaction triggers reminders of past conflicts. These may be events and experiences that occurred even before the relationship that resulted in similar feelings and took the person back to that space. This is often totally subconscious. For example: *My mom and dad frequently disappointed me, and so does my spouse.*

As you can see, people don't reason and discuss in a linear fashion; they move fluidly to different levels. They can be arguing at different levels over the same topic and feeling frustrated, exasperated, and hurt over the failure to resolve even simple things.

The most elegant work of a caregiver is to help two or more people do what they may not be able to do on their own: understand the different levels and the conversation behind the conversation.

Jesus often did this. Take, for example, His beautiful encounter with the woman at the well. She thought they were talking about literal water—the kind you drink. And, indeed, that's what they were talking about. Yet simultaneously, Jesus was talking about eternity and God and grace.

Eventually, she understood the conversation behind the conversation.

In the world of family and couples counseling, this is called systems thinking. It suggests that to solve a problem "here," you work "over there." You draw a large circle around the couple or the family or the parent and the child, and in every discussion, you converse with all parties. Systems thinking is found on every page in the biblical text. In Paul's letters, he was writing to a church or a region. And he was writing indirectly to everyone else—even to us, thousands of years later. When we think in terms of levels, we're able to help people get to the root of the conflict instead of merely scratching the surface.

Skill #6: Defining and Confronting Harmful Patterns

While less experienced lay listeners should not be the ones offering direct intervention to highly conflicted couples and families, everyone should have a broad grasp of basic issues and interventions. That way, the lay helper can recognize when certain potentially harmful patterns arise, know when something should be referred, and have a basic understanding of what more highly trained clinicians and coaches will do with those couples and families. And the pastor and coordinator, as overseers, can be aware of the depth, scope, and nature of how church members are counseled.

Because marriage mentoring, in particular, is such a common (and helpful) form of lay support, skill 6 focuses on marriage and romantic relationships. We should also note that many churches, along with much research, have discovered that lay efforts can be very effective with one caregiver and multiple couples in a group. As one counselor told us, "In my experience, the leader begins the session by bringing up a topic, and the couples themselves carry on most of the teaching, with only occasional leader intervention. (This works for relational and communications issues, but not for hardcore betrayals.)"

Here are a few factors every leader should be aware of.

Identifying External Patterns of Conflict

The most wide-reaching marital research in the twenty-first century has been done by John Gottman and his research team at the University of Washington. Hundreds of studies have emerged from his famous "Love Lab," an apartment overlooking Lake Washington in Seattle. More than three thousand couples have stayed in the Love Lab apartment for times of retreat and respite—under the observation of the Gottman team. Microphones and cameras are strategically placed in the apartment (but not in the bedroom or bathroom!) to record interactions. Couples have their vital signs (heart rate, blood pressure, respiration rate) monitored so the team can assess how couples manage tasks, become elevated in tension, and show capacity for restoration and reconciliation.

Gottman's team identified four harmful relationship patterns that caregivers can be trained to look for during conversations. Gottman calls these the "Four Horsemen of the Apocalypse." They are criticism, contempt, defensiveness, and stonewalling. A fifth pattern, flooding, is also important to recognize. Although Gottman's initial research was specifically about romantic relationships, it's helpful to identify these patterns in any type of relationship.[2]

Criticism is an attack on a person and their character. It's usually expressed with frustration, such as "You always . . ." or "Whenever I just [statement of innocence], you [statement of guilt]."

Contempt is an expression of meanness. This may be a sarcastic response, rolling the eyes, an intentional dig, or name-calling. This involves intentional humiliation; the goal is to back the other person away through a direct attempt to hurt them.

Defensiveness is the common response to criticism and/or contempt. Criticism is rarely received with gratitude and a humble promise to change. Rather, we tend to escalate with a self-protective response. We typically deflect the perceived attack and counter it by casting blame or avoiding responsibility.

Stonewalling is shutting down and shutting the other person out. This can be done when someone literally withdraws or when they remove themselves emotionally by not communicating. It conveys anything from icy coldness to condescension and often leaves the other person feeling insecure and utterly alone.

Flooding is evidenced when someone is emotionally overwhelmed (often by the first four ideas expressed above). While flooding is more common in men than women, both experience it. This can *look* like stonewalling, but it's different in intent. When someone's brain is emotionally flooded, they simply aren't able to access thoughts and words well. The frustration can be intense, especially if their partner continues to press forward for answers. The flooded person may walk away and slam the door on the way out.

Identifying Internal Patterns of Conflict

The one addition we would offer to these categories is something we've seen in our research and written about in our books (Jim in *Counseling Couples in Conflict* and Shaunti in her books about men and women, *For Women Only* and *For Men Only*). Statistically, men and women trend toward different patterns of insecurity, as well as different patterns of behavior once those insecurities are triggered. This is not universal, but it is common. When a raw nerve is hit, something can *feel* like criticism or contempt or a lack of love when the other person has no idea it's coming across that way.

For example, anger and withdrawal are common symptoms of pain, confusion, and heartache in men. These aren't necessarily signs of malice. A husband can dearly love his wife and still shut down when he feels hurt and confused. This looks like stonewalling, but it's much easier to unlock once both people have examined where they are (perhaps unintentionally) hitting each other's insecurities.

It's important for pastors and coordinators to prepare caregivers to be able to recognize the patterns in relational conflict so they can get them on the table and encourage both parties to address them. It's easy for caregivers to be pulled into the vortex of conflict because they don't recognize what's happening. Once patterns have been identified, it's possible to support alternative ways of interacting at a basic level. When the caregiver suspects a higher level of care for the couple is needed, they should consult with the coordinator.

Identifying Dangerous Patterns of Conflict

When it comes to recognizing dangerous patterns, it's also important to discuss the church's policies toward abuse, manipulation, and control. In our research, we found evidence of growth and progress in the church when it comes to addressing domestic or intimate partner violence—and evidence that the church still has far to go.

A 2018 Lifeway survey found that nearly all Protestant pastors (96 percent) were aware of resources to help address this problem. That encouraging finding showed a marked improvement since 2014, when only 61 percent of pastors were aware of resources. But that same study found that only 18 percent of pastors believed this was a problem occurring in their church.[3] In other words, "We know how to address the problem, but the problem isn't here. It's down the street at that other church."

There are many different statistics, sources, and methodologies related to intimate partner violence (or IPV), and it's difficult to determine an approximate prevalence. But evidence indicates that the number of victims in the US each year is in the millions. One report on the worldwide prevalence of IPV looked at multiple studies and included broad but common abuse factors such as coercion, control, and threatening behavior. The researchers found that among women over the age of fifteen around the world, 37 percent had experienced such maltreatment in their lifetime, with 24 percent experiencing it in the last year.[4]

Regardless of the exact numbers, domestic abuse in the US and abroad is far too common— and for women, that maltreatment is usually significantly more dangerous. It's vital for pastors to recognize that the church is not immune to manipulation, coercion, and violence. In any congregation, there may be women who are looking at the pastor and wondering, *Are you a safe person to talk to about my lack of safety at home?* Here are four suggestions for pastors and other leaders when it comes to abuse among people in the church:

1. Lay caregivers might play an important supportive role—they often discover manipulation, control, or abuse because they have created established, trusting relationships. But they won't always know what they are seeing—they just know something is "off." The pastor and coordinator will need to recognize and follow up when the caregiver says things like "It was so frustrating to be with them . . ." or "I know I am pretty good at what I do, but with this family, I felt so powerless . . ." Those expressions of futility are often the marker of need that goes beyond what volunteer caregivers are trained to handle. A clinician who is experienced and trained should be brought in to assess the potential for danger and even to make a plan for immediate safety if needed.
2. In situations where the church has predominantly male leadership and male-on-female abuse is suspected, female experts should be brought in to advise, gather information, and consult with pastors and leaders. Without women in roles of authority and protection, even a sincere attempt to understand the truth is often experienced by female victims as an untrustworthy setting.
3. When men are abusive, they need significant care to learn how to manage anger and how to attend to their own

healing. Men often make the mistake of seeing their primary goal as getting their family "back to normal." Pastors should lead men to see their goal as becoming healthy, secure, and capable of being strong *and* safe men.

4. Not all abuse is done by men. This is true of most physical abuse, but there are other types of mistreatment that should be considered. Selfish disregard for someone else may not be as visible, but it can be devastating as well. For example, consider a wife who has an intense desire to control everything her husband does, paired with constant contempt when her standards aren't met. Such a situation is inevitably destructive to the relationship. This can be particularly hurtful if no one—the church, their friends, or even the couple themselves—sees or addresses this pattern as the mistreatment it is.

Skill #7: Teaching Love and Respect in All Relationships

In our conversations about a Christian approach to different types of relationships—marriage, parenting, and so on—we have stressed the biblical concepts of love and respect, obedience and encouragement, grace and non-provocation.

These ideas are found in parallel passages in Ephesians 5–6 and Colossians 3. (Some readers will be familiar with the books Emerson Eggerichs has written on the "love and respect" ideas, in particular.[5])

In training others for relational care, we suggest that pastors focus on the foundational ideas found *before* the instruction on marriage in Ephesians 4 and Colossians 3:1-17.

Paul presents the foundation for healthy relationships in the church, in the workplace, and especially in the home. He then uses marriage, parenting, and labor as illustrations and applications for these ideas.

Caregivers in training are encouraged to study together the concept and outcome of Colossians 3:1-17 and Ephesians 4:1-6. Here we find powerful imagery drawn from the Trinity and applied to the church, marriage, and the family. Just as Jews spoke these words daily, "Hear, O Israel, the LORD our God, the LORD is one" (Deuteronomy 6:4), Jesus prayed to His Father that His followers would be one in Him, asking "that they may be one as we are one—I in them and you in me—so that they may be brought to complete unity" (John 17:22-23, NIV).

Paul reminds believers that it's through this concept of being united in love that followers of Christ know how to act. Ephesians 4:2 says, "Be completely humble and gentle; be patient, bearing with one another in love" (NIV). In a similar tone, he writes in Colossians 3:12-13, "As God's chosen people, holy and dearly loved, clothe yourselves with compassion, kindness, humility, gentleness and patience. Bear with each other and forgive one another if any of you has a grievance against someone" (NIV).

These characteristics are what make it possible to insert love and respect into the space between people, rather than barbs and bombs.

The goal of a caregiver's presence in a relationship where there has been a pattern of hurt, frustration, blame, or withdrawal is to lower the emotional intensity so that the parties can insert the biblical alternative. Love and respect can be experienced when compassion, kindness, humility, gentleness, and patience are demonstrated, along with other virtues.

Once the parties in a relationship turn from exhibiting the "four horsemen" to being willing to build up and encourage each other, the doors open to simple but helpful next steps. For example, my (Shaunti's) 30-Day Kindness Challenge is a simple and empirically tested three-step program to alter relational tensions in one month.[6] The results are often dramatic, because while the person thinks they're working on the relationship, they are actually working on themselves. And ultimately, that dynamic is what forms the core of a lay caregiver's role in working with a relationship.

While relational care can be a complicated endeavor, it's also a very important ministry of the church. So often, relationships simply need a third person who is willing to help each person untangle *themselves* and provide stability, accountability, and encouragement. And that's where a caregiver can step in. Mature relationships may take hard work to create, but supportive lay mentors and caregivers can be highly effective toward this goal.

11

Addressing Addictions

Relying on God's Power When We Are Powerless

The men and women who are truly filled with light are those who have gazed deeply into the darkness of their own imperfect existence.

BRENNAN MANNING, *The Furious Longing of God*

Some things are just ideal. If you want to eat the perfect baguette, it has to be in Paris. If you want to see the most world-changing art, travel to Florence. If you're going to run one marathon, make it Boston. While you can eat, see, or run anywhere, some places are just the best.

If you're going to be serious about overcoming addiction and temptation, you'll go to church. The message of the gospel meets the experience of every person and exceeds the standards of addiction recovery, for four key reasons.

First, the gospel declares that people are powerless. Try as we might to achieve, control, and succeed, we all fail. If we're willing to be honest with ourselves, all of us will ultimately concede that we can't control ourselves, our circumstances, and our outcomes.

For everyone facing addiction, including every follower of Jesus, this is where we start. Paul's cry in Romans 7 is the realization of every person on the path to recovery: "What a wretched man I am! Who will rescue me from this body that is subject to death?" (verse 24, NIV).

The second key is God. In our condition of realized powerlessness, we know there is a God who loves us, cares for us, and protects us. This knowledge prompts Paul, in the next verse, to drop to his knees and say, "Thanks be to God, who delivers me through Jesus Christ our Lord!" (Romans 7:25, NIV).

The third key is the need to connect the first idea with the second: our powerlessness with the One who is all-powerful. It's not enough to realize our vulnerability or powerlessness. Nor is it enough to know that God is capable. The gap between our inadequacy and God's potency must be brought together. In many addiction traditions, it is the group that supplies the impetus to connect the person with a "higher power."

This power is Jesus. Because of His humanity and His deity, our inadequacy meets God's capability. And it is in the church, the community of saints, where both are shared, realized, and demonstrated. The church prompts, encourages, confronts, and supports the individual toward worship of God, and helps members of the group uphold one another in the pursuit of holiness.

Finally, there is purpose. Because of who we are and who Jesus is, we can have a redefined and renewed purpose. For those who want to be healed and delivered from addiction, the paradox is that we are empowered by our powerlessness and our reliance on God's power, accessed through the Cross. People going through addiction recovery understand, often intimately, the truths of the Christian journey.

This chapter focuses on what church leaders need to know so they can make certain key decisions. The goal is for the church to be able to speak effectively into the lives of those on the addiction recovery journey, whether that's a teenager dependent on pot, a woman who confesses that she "has" to drink three glasses of alcohol each night to feel okay, or a man broken by his inability to stop looking at porn.

Like the other chapters, we have seven skills—or perhaps seven steps. (Twelve steps would be more appropriate, but that was already taken by another group. Maybe consider this chapter the seven steps to use the twelve steps in your church!)

Skill #1: Understanding Addiction, and What the Church Can Do

Here, we discuss how the church can help with addictions, which includes addictive behaviors that cause distress and wreck relationships. But it should be noted that the Diagnostic and Statistical Manual of Mental Disorders (the manual that outlines the criteria for a mental health diagnosis) does not include most behavioral addictions (for example, sexual addiction) as diagnosable conditions. This doesn't mean that behavioral addictions don't exist; it just means that according to the prevailing view of the current research, there isn't enough evidence to classify them as a medical condition.

As we've already discussed, many recovery programs that address addiction also go beyond traditional notions of addiction and into "hurts, habits, or hang-ups" that we need help working through. This chapter, however, focuses solely on the traditional concept of addiction: when we're controlled by anything we put in our body or mind, or anything we compulsively do as a result. This can be an addiction to drugs, alcohol, smoking, or food; the rush of gambling, shopping, erotica, pornography; or many other things. The key is that the addiction keeps us stuck in a cycle that diverts our attention from other life concerns and leaves us constantly wanting more of something that can't address our deepest need.

Because of the wide array of addictive issues your church will likely encounter, this topic has both some flexibility (which we will cover here) and some stringency (which we will cover in skill #2).

There are many helpful models and programs available, some of which (such as Celebrate Recovery) address almost any type of recovery and some of which are extremely issue specific (such as a support group for those with eating disorders or a pornography compulsion). We consider many of these programs to be part of the trained helper layer of the triangle because they're led by someone who has gone through robust training and often has experience in the area themselves.

There are also multiple options for the lay listener level. Many churches have men's accountability groups. Others may pull together a temporary small group for women who are trying to kick the habit of that second and third glass of wine in the evening. Yet others may form a discipleship group for youth who want support in dealing with a particular struggle. The opportunities are endless; the key is that a church must have a mechanism for funneling people into lay support where it exists and creating a system where it doesn't.

Skill #2: Understanding Addiction, and What the Church Cannot Do

Despite the variety and flexibility for care options, there are also some strict protocols. And there's good reason for this, because addictions are dangerous. But not all the danger is equal. Asphyxia from an opioid overdose or a liver destroyed by alcohol can kill you. An online shopping addiction that you hide from your spouse is destructive but not deadly. It's possible to rebuild a credit score or a marriage, but one can't undo a damaged liver.

All lay caregivers must be prepared to identify people who need more than a warm conversation and encouragement—they urgently need to be transitioned to a place of safety, where they can get clinical help. Not everyone needs hospitalized detoxification, but some people do. For those who don't know they need it, the lay caregiver and church leadership can recognize this for them.

The more dangerous an issue is—to someone's life, marriage, career, or children—the more likely it is that the issue should *not* be substantively addressed in a one-on-one lay setting. A lay counselor, listener, small group leader, or coach is rarely the right option to help someone deep in the throes of addiction. They simply aren't equipped with the technical knowledge and steps that need to be taken. For example, suppose a lay counselor learns that the person they've seen three times lied on the intake form and is still snorting cocaine. The layperson must instantly grasp that this person needs a higher level of help than they can provide.

That individual needs to be immediately referred to a professional—either an appropriate therapist or a professional program that's equipped to help them. The church would do that person a disservice by trying to counsel them with technical steps to get free from the addiction.

That said, the church must not overlook that there *are* things church caregivers can do to support the person who is referred onward. Depending on the situation, the person might be connected to the prayer ministry, a one-on-one accountability partner, and/or someone to stay in touch with them while they're in a rehab program. They could be connected to the person who runs the recovery ministry so that when time comes for recovery, they can quickly become part of that supportive community.

There are abundant resources designed for caregiving nonprofessionals that explain crucial concepts that will help, such as how addictive behaviors form and what's happening in the brain of someone who has addictive patterns. Not only is a simple understanding helpful for caregivers, but it also highlights the church as a place for accurate information.

For example, people commonly refer to "chemical imbalances" in the brain, when that's generally a misleading metaphor for the highly complex (and still not completely understood) reality of what's going on in the mind and body of someone with an addiction. This analogy is especially incomplete since mental health is different from other physical processes that we call "chemical imbalances," such as those that cause organ malfunction. An imbalance in your kidney doesn't respond when you talk to it. A better analogy may be that the brain's chemical and cellular factory simply isn't working properly, but it can often be improved through interpersonal and clinical interventions.

As you can see, there is a wide array of possibilities and ways to support the needs of those with addictions who seek the care and protection of the church community. We suggest that pastors seek the guidance and expertise of addiction professionals to assist in creating church-based interventions.

Skill #3: Knowing the Territory

Recovery work is one of the most meaningful lay-led ways to help people in need of care and discipleship. As we mentioned earlier, those who have been in recovery are often looking to give back and may be some of a church's most motivated volunteers. Yet while the core messages are parallel, the typical church culture of care and the addiction culture of care are often very different. Traditional addiction care (especially when it comes to drugs and alcohol) has a language, rituals, and a code that can easily lead to misunderstanding and competition with the church.

As the church starts to offer certain areas of care, leaders must recognize and be okay with the fact that they will be venturing into a different sort of territory.

First, especially in the arena of substance abuse, allegiance to "the program" and process is very strong for those whose lives are changed through their recovery. In particular, for many in recovery, there's a perception that only an addict can help an addict. Also, in most recovery arenas (perhaps in contrast to the beliefs of other people in the congregation), there's an understanding that, as the saying goes, "relapse is part of recovery." If you mess up, you figure out why, get accountability to help you overcome whatever tripped you up, and move forward. There's very little judgment for messing up, because addicts understand the struggle.

Second, there's often a feeling in the recovery space that churches are for "nice" people who think they're doing pretty well. And we may need to acknowledge that there's a reason for that perception. Church culture tends to acknowledge sins someone *used to* struggle with. Recovery culture looks for and acknowledges sins someone is struggling with today. For some people, it feels as if the broader church is shaming, while recovery groups are safe.

Thus, one of the most important tasks for pastors in response to these perceptions is to lead the church in creating a welcoming, nonjudgmental context that is okay with some of the quirks of these programs and sees the overall need with clear eyes while not being thrown by it. In a way, it's a whole-church version of the calm, accepting presence that is the key to caring listening.

Skill #4: Knowing Your Response to Each Category of Need

In nonprofessional settings, we use the word *addiction* to mean a lot of different things. Looking at this chart, consider these increasing levels of severity used to describe addictions: *first use*, *regular use*, *risky use* or *misuse*, *abuse*, *dependence*, *disordered use*. Although this general pattern is helpful for understanding and making decisions about care for all addictions and behavioral compulsions, these specific categories are particularly targeted to substance abuse disorders.

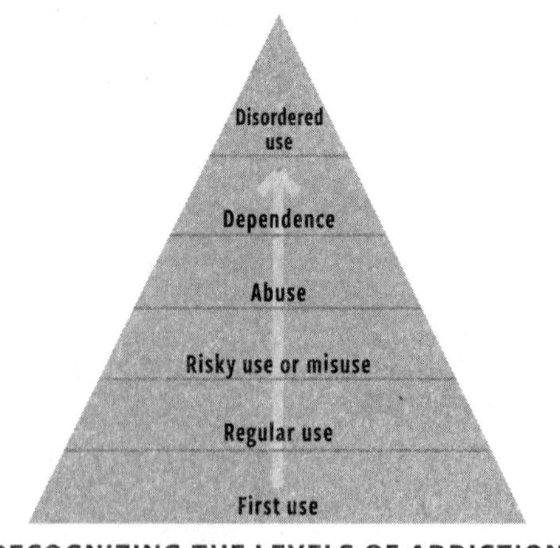

RECOGNIZING THE LEVELS OF ADDICTION

Each phrase connotes that the person is under a greater and greater degree of control by the substance, with perhaps less and less control over their life. However, for most chemical and behavioral addictions, the experience of getting there differs from person to person. First use doesn't always lead to regular use. For example, an initial use of drugs or alcohol (or porn or gambling) isn't necessarily a "gateway" to more severe use. But everyone—no matter the severity—starts with a first use. Delaying first use during adolescence or young adulthood means that someone has greater protection from more severe levels later.

The question for the leader is, at what threshold does the church trigger a referral to a professional program or therapist?

Here are considerations to help you make that decision.

The first three stages are still concerning, but they provide lots of opportunities for prevention and early intervention—which can, depending on the situation, be great avenues for lay care. We cover more of this later in the chapter.

The last three stages, however, have legal and medical implications that the initial stages do not. This is one reason we recommend that churches strongly consider referring people to professionals and to certified programs and people beginning at this point.

Despite how we tend to use it, *abuse* is a medical term. It means continued use despite known and recognized problems caused by its use. For example, suppose a person has been confronted three times about missing work. Unbeknownst to the employer, it was because of hangovers from partying the night before. One more incident, and the person will be fired. It's early Monday morning—1:15 a.m.—and they're drinking like it's New Year's Eve. And they're scheduled to be at work at 8:00 that morning. That meets the technical definition of substance abuse. This is the type of situation that a pastor, a coordinator, or a lay caregiver could become aware of.

The next two levels, dependence and disorder, are technically separate, but for our purposes we'll discuss them together. Dependence is measured by the need to have an increased amount to get the same effect. Some people are proud of the fact that they can now drink ten cans of beer and it hardly phases them at all. To their drinking buddies, that may be something they cheer. But to the medical community, it's evidence of a body that has accommodated to the drug. They actually may be as intoxicated as the novice drinker; they're just less aware of the drug's effect.

A dependence-like pattern is also common with behavioral compulsions such as pornography use (although, again, in medical terms, it's not considered an addiction), where someone feels the need to consume more and more hardcore content to get the same effect. Regardless of the issue, as use trends into these two stages, the person's life, career, and relationships are increasingly in jeopardy. That said, the consequences depend on the actual substance. A smoker can be completely dependent on nicotine but living a functional life, whereas a person dependent on opioids is likely to be destroying their life, career, marriage, and family.

As leaders of the church community, pastors can establish how the church will engage addictions and up to what level. What sort of situations can be addressed primarily by a recovery ministry? At what point does the church refer out—and to what kind of professional or program? And how does the church continue to care for the person in need?

Remember, these issues are *already* in the church—and probably at frequencies similar to the rate in the general community. Thoughtful leadership, often with the guidance of a professional who understands addictions, will help establish the most effective care.

Skill #5: Assessing the Personal Level of Need

Soon after someone is welcomed into any type of care, a common phrase is "We're glad you're here. What's going on, and how can we help?" In the clinical world, we call that assessment. In the ministry world, it's "Tell us your story."

A church coordinator or lay caregiver will probably not do a comprehensive behavioral history or conduct formal testing. But a short intake tool to learn about the addictive situation is helpful. This may include amount, length of use, frequency, and patterns so the more dangerous conditions can be identified and referred out. Just be aware that people often describe their addictive patterns inaccurately, minimize them, or deny them altogether early in the interaction. Information gained at the outset is important, but it should be taken with a grain of salt.

Accurate assessment usually becomes possible once there's an absence of shame. And shame reduction takes time, because it's associated with trust and safety.

A good ministry-based assessment should be presented in simple, easy, nonformal language. Examples of good church assessments can be found in many places; you don't have to invent one. Some are available at Thechurchcares.com and can be edited to each ministry's need.

In general, this type of intake assessment should include the many parts of a person's identity, including (1) the physical (their body),

(2) the emotional (their affective well-being or mental health), (3) the spiritual (their beliefs and experiences about God and eternity), (4) the social (their relationships, family, friends, and environment), and (5) the immediate details of life.

Assessments exist to allow both the person in need of care and the church leaders (and caregivers) to make appropriate decisions. Being aware of the needs and how to connect people to the best pathways to healing—inside and outside the church—is essential. For example, someone with even a moderate level of an eating disorder absolutely needs medical care as part of their portfolio of support.

Skill #6: Being Equipped with the Basics

We've talked a lot about the areas of addiction lay caregivers should *not* try to address—those areas and levels where active substance use is increasingly dangerous to someone's life, relationships, and work. But as you look again at the "Recognizing the Levels of Addiction" chart in skill 4, you'll remember that there are three "starter" levels where active substance use has a lower risk to health and well-being. And there is also an additional category to consider: courageous individuals who confront their addiction through recovery, one day at a time. These individuals should also continue to seek support.

Churches ask, "What do we actually do at the lay caregiver level of the CARE triangle?" (see chapter 1). We are not a treatment center (the top of the triangle). We already have Celebrate Recovery or other ministry programs that focus on addictions (the middle of the triangle). What can be done by lay listeners (at the base of the triangle)?"

The answer is an essential part of care: the lay caregiver—for example, perhaps an accountability partner or a volunteer facilitator in a discussion group—can help the person in recovery or less-dangerous addiction levels secure their commitment to making change. The lay caregiver can then offer support as the person forms good habits to replace harmful ones. The metaphor of entering a home is a way to understand how the church supports those addressing addiction at this most basic level.

The welcome stage. The person steps through the front door and receives "front hall" affirmation and support—the equivalent of a warm welcome and a handshake or a hug. The message being delivered is "We're glad you are here! You've made a great choice in joining us. We get you. This is where you belong. Let us introduce you to everyone else."

At this welcoming stage, the lay caregiver uses listening skills to help the person move away from defensiveness and blame. Affirmation reinforces and supports the person's understanding of their problem. ("Steve, it's great that you see how your porn problem might be impacting your marriage. You made the right choice to join our group.") It also explicitly allows the person to acknowledge their awareness of their need and to make a life change.

The awareness of options stage. Next, the guest proceeds down a hallway with multiple doors—sort of like the multiple options in front of the person wrestling with addiction. The lay caregiver helps the person form an awareness of their options and make some decisions about what they're going to do. Imagine the host saying, "This door leads to the family room, where some people are hanging out. The bathroom is that first door on the left. The door on the right is the kitchen, if you want to help prepare the meal. Make yourself at home."

In addiction care and recovery, there are many possible "doors." The person must consider whether to address problems in life (for example, job stress, a breakup, or separation from family) that accelerate addictive behaviors. They might need to face weighty emotions. They might need to consider harmful habits and life patterns, including substance use, pornography, gambling, or patterns of chronic underachievement. Church caregivers can offer support as the person selects which door they want to start with.

The summarizing and action stage. Finally, the lay caregiver helps the person engage in summarizing and action. Using the house metaphor, the person goes to a given room and gets to work. Others are in that room, too, doing that same work—as are lay caregivers who might be there for fellowship, support, or prayer. People working through addiction and recovery need others at each step and transition. In this stage, the church joins the person with productive, supportive activity that will help them get where they want to be.

Addiction recovery can be a life journey. It's good to have friends and to have a place to be at home. That is what the church and lay caregivers provide.

Skill #7: Allowing Addictions Care to Teach the Church

The Christian gospel—and the work of discipleship—is woven into the fabric of addictions care. Christians carry three redemptive messages. First, we are broken. Second, we are healed. Third, we carry the paradox of being healed yet broken. This message is central to recovery culture—and it's something that can be taught to the broader church. We find that pastors who embrace this message and/or those who have journeyed through it themselves form environments where churches embrace the humility of John Newton, who wrote the song "Amazing Grace." In the movie about his life, he's quoted as saying, "Although my memory's fading, I remember two things very clearly: I am a great sinner and Christ is a great Savior."[1]

It's not a coincidence that addiction culture has captured the word *recovery*. And the term is used in the present tense. A person says, "I am in recovery," not "I have recovered," "I am going to recover," or "I was recovered, but now I'm not."

The message from those in recovery to the broader church is that, as Christians, we are redeemed yet remain broken and in need of grace. We are held together securely, but parts of our journey may always feel tenuous—one day at a time. Through working in this wide and diverse area of addictions and recovery—an area that will touch a significant percentage of the people in your congregation at one time or another—the church will develop both a crucial skill and a crucial attitude. Paul describes it directly in Galatians 6:1, where we are to "restore that person gently" (NIV). But in verses 1 and 2 we are also told, "Watch yourselves, or you also may be tempted. Carry each other's burdens, and in this way you will fulfill the law of Christ" (NIV).

The broad theme that the Galatians learned—as will we, when we walk in addictions ministry—is that families, churches, and communities have the high calling of developing, nurturing, and restoring those within their care. We are not to isolate the few who are identified as "unclean" but to become the agents of healing for all—ourselves included. Our hope is that pastors will set the theology of addiction from the pulpit and help *all* those in their church understand that we'll never be "good enough," but there is One who is.

12

Addressing Trauma and Grief

Walking with Others Through Mourning to Meaning

I think a look at suffering humanity would lead to the realization that trauma is perhaps the greatest mission field of the twenty-first century.

DIANE LANGBERG, *Suffering and the Heart of God*

The prophet Isaiah proclaimed a vision for "the year of the LORD's favor" (Isaiah 61:2). Almost a millennium later, on a Sabbath in the synagogue in Nazareth, Jesus stood and read part of Isaiah 61:

The Spirit of the Sovereign LORD is on me,
because the LORD has anointed me
to proclaim good news to the poor.
He has sent me to bind up the brokenhearted,
to proclaim freedom for the captives
and release from darkness for the prisoners . . .
to bestow on them a crown of beauty
instead of ashes,

the oil of joy
  instead of mourning,
and a garment of praise
  instead of a spirit of despair.
They will be called oaks of righteousness,
  a planting of the Lord
  for the display of his splendor.

ISAIAH 61:1, 3, NIV

The metaphor of oaks of righteousness offers an elegant description of the work of caregivers. They are tree planters, but in a special context. Isaiah describes the brokenhearted, the poor, and the captives. These oaks of righteousness were being planted in a land that knew disaster. The once fruitful land was treeless and barren, charred and decimated. Just like so many who have endured trauma and great grief.

The traumas people have endured might stem from a single event—like a fire that takes out a whole forest. Or it can come as the result of a long-term decline—like diseases that spread and kill one tree at a time over decades.

But where disaster and blight have struck, we—with the help of Jesus—can grow forests!

In this chapter, we share the seven skills caregivers need to sit with people in trauma and grief. These two types of pain carry unique characteristics. Both exist after an uprooting or a destruction of what was once safe and stable. Trauma and grief show "outside/inside" characteristics. Something occurs outside (a disaster, an accident, death, loss, violence, or another painful circumstance), and this event prompts the brain to react "inside," in self-protection mode.

Skill #1: Know the Focus of Trauma Care

The purpose of care in the aftermath of trauma or grief is reorientation. People tend to mark and define their existence by major events, just as cultures and generations do. For example, the Greatest Generation might ask, "Where were you when you learned of the Pearl Harbor attack?" Boomers could inquire, "Where were you when JFK or Martin Luther King Jr. were assassinated?" Most today can consider, "Where were you on 9/11?" These events are social traumas.

In a similar way, individual trauma and grief are seared into our memory. They even cause us to mark time. Life can be defined by these points on the calendar: before and after. And we easily define *ourselves* through these events as well.

Yet when Jesus spoke the words of Isaiah 61, there was world-defining change in orientation. To be freed, healed, or released through Jesus is to no longer see these shattering events as the defining moments in our life. Rather, they are seen as drastically important incidents that we never would have chosen but can be used to shape and direct us to a greater purpose.

It's crucial for caregivers to understand this as the goal of trauma and grief care. Healing from trauma or grief means developing the ability to carry the events of the past and to bear the weight of the loss *without* experiencing despair or imprisonment.

For many who experience crushing situations, there's a type of captivity that takes place, in which the memory of the event dominates the sufferer's daily thought processes. The person is in a prison that they feel incapable of getting out of. The goal of the caregiver is to help the person be released from that prison. In most cases, the person will, in time, be able to bear the real weight of these events, along with the thoughts and emotions that come with them, without being crushed or consumed by them. The ultimate goal is to regain the ability to live in contentment.

Note that the goal is not to "take away" sadness or other negative emotions that come up. As noted in chapter 9, our emotions serve a purpose. For example, victims of violence will—and probably should—carry a somewhat heightened awareness of danger. A better way to understand the goal is to help the person get to peace when danger isn't present.

Think about a glitchy home electric generator that produces electricity 24-7, with constant squeals and rumbles, and doesn't put itself into sleep mode when the demand for electricity is lower. During the night it is still running (and squealing), and you just can't sleep. It simply won't turn off.

A brain that has gone through trauma may always be on "danger watch," running full tilt even at times when it should instead be experiencing safety, healing, and calm. The goal of good care is to help the person "turn down the engine" when the demand is lower. There may be a need for specialized therapy or medical intervention (for example, certain types of stimulation help the brain rewire itself), but there is often much that the lay community can do as well.

Leading the caregivers in your church community to become trauma informed and to be able to walk others through the "valley of the shadow of death" is among the loveliest and most Christlike tasks of any church. Many resources are available for getting advanced lay certification in trauma care (for example, through the American Bible Society's Trauma Research Institute) or for developing a disaster ministry through groups such as the Humanitarian Disaster Institute. You can see all these resources at Thechurchcares.com.

Skill #2: Be Present in Grief and Mourning

The book of Job teaches us much about how to care for the grieving and the traumatized. It offers examples of paths that heal and those that cause harm. The most important lesson learned from Job is, essentially, "Shut up and listen!"

As we've already noted, this is among the most difficult lessons for both the new caregiver and the advanced clinician. No matter the level of expertise, there's a constant pull toward trying to ease suffering through magic words. While demonstrating a listening presence is important in all situations, it's most important when there has been loss or a threat to safety.

Some people misunderstand the directive "Shut up and listen" to mean that we're to do nothing, say nothing. Like a human statue. But it's wrong to suggest that good listening in the presence of trauma means offering silence—like a vacuum of space, void of content. You may have noticed that creating emptiness only increases anxiety. Rather, being emotionally present means recognizing which kind of words are helpful—and which aren't. The most powerful words are when we simply ask the grieving to share their memories and experiences. When we say, "I'm so sorry." Powerful words of care can be delivered in a few short minutes—but the effects last for days, or even a lifetime.

Think of the power of a friend bringing paper products to a home that's in mourning. The very brief words are "I thought people might be coming by. I didn't want you to have to wash dishes. Here are plates, cups, and plasticware. You are loved. We grieve with you."

Lay listeners and trained helpers in the context of the church can have similar messages as they are simply present with someone who is grieving or dealing with the aftereffects of trauma.

Pastors and coordinators oversee the formation of these skills through conversation and planning. Even more than in other arenas, people are mentored in the art of compassion in the presence of loss. People can work in teams, with the novice caregiver observing and participating with someone who is more experienced.

Skill #3: Think of Who and Where God Was, Before, During, and After

The fundamental questions that come with all grief and trauma—and to some degree with *all* the pain and distress we've discussed in this book—are "Where was God?" and "How could God let this happen to me?"

There are many ways the church can teach caregivers how to respond when people are experiencing pain and are searching for reasons. But ultimately, every Christian caregiver will (hopefully) have the same goal as part of the healing process, which was described well by a church leader who trains lay caregivers in trauma response. She said, "In our endeavors, a caregiver's role is to help a lamenting person see Jesus in their pain, help them stand firm on truths about God instead of being tossed by the waves of their emotions, and help them move from an unhealthy perspective to a perspective that allows them to see God's fingerprints—how He *is* showing up and helping, offering rescue and healing. Over time, the hope is that they will even see how God can bring beauty from ashes."

The first response to a lament is to stay with the person in pain as they're experiencing suffering and wondering why. In other words, being what Job's friends *should* have been: present, without the condemning advice. But what does "staying" and being together look like, if we're supposed to be present, yet without either extreme of offering trite platitudes or becoming unhelpfully passive?

Imagine that you're sitting with a twenty-five-year-old mother whose husband died a week ago. Being together may mean simply saying, "I grieve with you," then going on a walk and waiting to see what topic she raises. Being together might mean asking, "How did you and your husband face hard things?" Or "What do you know from the Bible about how you can respond to this grief? What about that seems real to you right now—or very distant?" Or even more practical questions, such as "This is a long journey. What must be addressed now, and what can wait for a while?"

It's a dialogue that gradually reorients both sufferer and caregiver toward being part of God's redemptive plan, and seeing God's presence even in painful events.

In their work on theological perspectives toward trauma, theologian Richard Langer and his colleagues suggest that caregivers help those in pain work through four questions:

1. Why me?
2. Where is God?
3. Where are my friends?
4. How long will it last?[1]

These questions are the laments of the prophet Jeremiah and are not meant to be answered by the caregiver. Rather, lay caregivers who want to serve in this arena will be trained on how to walk someone through these questions.

Because suffering is so painful, it's easy for the suffering person to respond to the four questions in these ways:

1. This is unfair, because those who are innocent should not suffer.
2. God is absent.
3. Friends have abandoned me.
4. The suffering will have no end.

Langer and his colleagues suggest that the conversation instead be directed toward the grace and hope of the gospel. We suggest that this includes these understandings:

1. We live in a sinful and fallen world, which painfully impacts each of us—but we can overcome the imprisonment of pain because Jesus has overcome the world (John 16:33).
2. God is always with us and at work in the suffering, even when our finite minds can't comprehend how—including by creating in us the character to walk with grace and trust God to redeem the suffering,
3. We, the church, are with you now! Other friends may be absent because they don't know what to say, not because they don't care. We can help you and your friends learn to face suffering together.

4. Suffering is for a season, during which His grace will get us through each day (2 Corinthians 12:9) and in which we know that one day God will wipe away every tear from our eyes (Revelation 21:3-4).

As caregivers walk the suffering person through those questions and considerations, they can help those in pain bend their experience toward meaning in light of God's purpose. Together, both the caregiver and the one in need can be inspired by examples in Scripture and the stories of others who saw purpose in pain. Job summarized this idea in Job 13:15 (NIV): "Though he slay me, yet will I hope in him." The realization that suffering can be purposeful and that the sufferer is not alone is usually the greatest comfort.

Skill #4: Implement Faith-Filled Coping Skills

Although the effects of trauma and grief are painful, there are many faith-filled skills that people can learn—both to cope with pain without creating a worse spiral and to move toward healing.

Ken Pargament, a prominent authority on the psychology of faith and religion, studied religious coping for decades. He found that positive religious coping led to better health, better outcomes after loss, and an increase in spiritual maturity.[2] He also found that there are five faith-filled skills that support healing. These are all skills a lay caregiver can help someone learn. They are:

1. Seeing meaning in the pain. (More on this below.)
2. Developing a sense of control over a troubling situation,

rather than a sense of helplessness. Taking action creates healing; even small symbolic acts promote health.

3. Praying and worshiping with others. Comfort is found in disciplines of worship, praise, and gratitude to God.
4. Simply being with others.
5. Redirecting the present pain toward future goals. One CARE-type program director told us, "We always say to the person we are working with, 'What can you do with this? What is your next step?'" Many caregivers will identify with this. Most who seek to be helpful to others have themselves been broken, grieved, or suffered trauma. Part of their healing involved being able to comfort others.

Skill #5: Make Meaning

The Langer piece mentioned earlier cites Paul Claudel as saying, "Happy is he who suffers and knows why."[3] Suffering without meaning creates despair and cynicism. But a great deal of research has found that hope and motivation often rise as we see suffering in the context of mission and purpose. For example: "This really hurts now, but maybe one day I'll be able to help others who are going through something similar."

The process of grief and trauma care (of all care, really) is to travel with, partner with, and be present with another in their pain. The caregiver ultimately offers a *process*, not a measurable product or a solution in five easy steps. And this process involves making meaning out of what has occurred. What might God be doing during this time following the trauma or grief? How can we lean into what that is and survive it without being crushed? Meaning is made when the pain from life is exposed to the beauty of God's creation, the hope of God's promises, and the love of God's people.

This primarily occurs when fellow sojourners engage in these ideas and talk about them together. The church can help people move out of their individual silos of pain and journey with one another. The fellowship and connection found in church community are essential for making this possible.

There are many resources that will help, including at The Church Cares resource page. It's particularly valuable for those who have gone through trauma and grief themselves to be recruited as leaders; they can learn from the resources and become familiar with the technical content just as they are already aware of people's heart needs. Great lay leaders and caregivers are those who have explored their own pain and have come to accept that they're powerless to prevent the pain of others but are placed in the path of someone else's suffering to help unlock their transformation.

Skill #6: Partner with Specialists

In professional psychotherapy we refer to trauma and complex trauma. And we refer to grief and complicated grief. Pastors and coordinators must understand the difference between these and be prepared to partner with specialists as needed.

Here's a brief overview. Almost everyone has experienced some form of trauma and grief, but not all trauma and grief are pathological. The US Department of Veterans Affairs says, "The word *trauma* is used for many different types of experiences that are stressful. But not all stressful events are the type of trauma that can lead to PTSD." They go on to say that while it's most likely that everyone experiences a traumatic event, only about 6 percent of adults will develop PTSD at some point in their life (and many will recover and no longer experience symptoms).[4]

The church caregiver can and should be present in the lives of those who experience trauma and grief. And in complex circumstances, so should a professional therapist. The observant and aware coordinator, pastor, or caregiver, along with supportive loved ones who walk daily with those in pain, should be watching for signs that advanced intervention is needed. In other words, the caregiver—under the supervision of the coordinator—must be able to differentiate pain from trauma, and grief from complex responses such as PTSD.

For example, someone with prolonged grief disorder shows an inability to move beyond the loss after about a year. Caregivers should be aware when someone is "stuck" in this way. Most people who go through common grief exhibit powerful and deeply felt emotional responses—yet while the loss can be extremely painful, in most cases, they experience healthy lament. When the lament stage persists and appears to take permanent residence in the person's life patterns, however, they may need clinical or medical attention.

Similarly, someone with PTSD has, as a condition of the diagnosis, directly experienced or witnessed traumatic events, learned of traumatic experiences of family or friends, or repeatedly been exposed to extreme events or circumstances. This is followed by recurrent memories or dreams, or reexperiencing the circumstances as if they're still under threat. They may exhibit characteristics such as hypervigilance, fixation on events in the past, diminished interest in activities that would typically produce contentment, and an out-of-body sensation like *This is not happening to me.*

When there's prolonged reaction to trauma—suggesting the presence of a disorder—the person should be referred to a clinical expert, counselor, or psychologist who specializes in trauma reactions and who can conduct an assessment.

Trauma, especially, has become a specialized field. It's extremely valuable for pastors and coordinators to have these providers among their contacts for consultation and referral purposes.

Because of their presence in the lives of the injured, lay caregivers are often in the best position to suggest and pursue additional support, regardless of the issue. This amplifies rather than diminishes the importance of the lay caregiver and the importance of training so they can recognize when it's simple pain versus complex pain.

The lay levels of the church triangle are also vital for helping to *prevent* complex trauma and grief in the form of supportive conversations in one-on-one and group relationships. Ministries such as GriefShare[5] and trauma- and grief-informed small group Bible studies offered by the American Bible Society[6] can help caregivers participate in the healing process and prevent life pain from escalating into clinical disorders.

Skill #7: Teach and Model a Willingness to Access Support

In our experience working with churches, one of the most essential (and sometimes difficult) tasks is for caregivers and leaders to be willing to model what it looks like to access the support when it's needed.

And we are wrapping up not just this chapter but part 2 of the book with this step, because it applies not just to trauma and grief but to *all* the issues addressed in the book.

Many people want to help, but when they're experiencing crisis themselves, they are unlikely to seek help. All of us know the feeling: "I don't want to be a bother." A primary task for the church is to preach, teach, and model "needfulness." In other words, acknowledging that each person has needs and that each person benefits from rehearsing how to ask.

I (Jim) once heard a pastor declare in a sermon, "Ask yourself whether you have a personal need—something that is always catching your attention—that no other person knows about because you haven't shared it. You should be alarmed. Your self-contained remedy is probably worse than the actual need!" We concur.

Being able to express our need to a community begins with the pastor demonstrating how it's done. This doesn't mean they have to talk about personal trauma from the stage (although they can!). But a pastor can openly declare, "I share the details of my life stress, my discouragement, my pride, my fear, and my anxiety with a few trusted friends—and I encourage you to do so too."

If a leader struggles to say those words, then that's the place to start—both out of personal need and to build the essential foundation for healing within the congregation. Vulnerability declared by leadership will make it safer for the trauma victim to seek help. The leaders of groups that meet for Bible study and prayer can be encouraged to practice vulnerability as well. Those leaders can then ask participants to practice it too. At the outset, this can be explored in small, noninvasive ways. For example, "I have to confess: I don't know how to change the oil in my car. Can anyone teach me?" or "I have never been able to get on an exercise program and stick with it. Can anyone join me?"

The goal is to create a culture where people ask for someone to come alongside them regularly. Doing so will help everyone go deeper into some important reasons why they don't.

One church we're aware of trained dozens of lay helpers, but very few people in the church came forward to access the help—even though the leaders knew the need was there. The church investigated and identified that people's discomfort and hesitancy were rooted in pride and self-sufficiency. Clearly, that was just as important to address as the needs of people in pain!

Their innovative solution was to announce to the church that they had many trained helpers who, before they could be approved to meet with people with real needs, had to practice, meeting four times with people to hone their helping skills. The pastor asked the church, "Would you be willing to talk about your needs so these caregivers can be released to help others?" That pastor understood the idea of "thinking differently." The helpers got their practice, and a culture of pursuing help was created.

CONCLUSION

Equipping the Church to Transform the World

Recall the story of Robert Raikes and the Sunday school revolution he helped start. With the ordinary laypeople in his ordinary church, the compassion of God was released—and it changed the world. Not many people know Raikes's name, but untold generations have been impacted by him and the Christians of his day. And because you are reading this, that probably includes you.

There are many great movements of God's Spirit happening around us. Clean water. Bible translation. Child sponsorship. Creation care. International promotions of peace. Racial justice. Evangelism and world missions.

Among the most powerful movements in this second quarter of the twenty-first century is the attention toward mental health care. After hearing about this book, a respected Christian psychologist commented,

"For our time, the church has the attention of the world. A world that is hungry and thirsty for the message of the gospel delivered through relational care."

Robert Raikes had his moment. Now we have ours.

We see four important truths about the culture and the church today that make care ministries an important part of every church.

Truth #1: Mental health is a primary language in our culture—which gives the church an opportunity to be the translator.

Our era is characterized by the near obsession with how we feel. Demand for therapy, medication, healing retreats, and "three steps to fix your marriage" is at an all-time high. Some of the most popular videos on any social media platform are those that dive into whether a particular symptom or feeling is an indication of a mental health condition. Is my desire to avoid that dinner party a sign of social anxiety disorder? Your husband's attitude is clearly a signal of narcissism. Here's how ADHD changes your brain.

That's not to say that those presentations are bad! In fact, many of them are extremely helpful—even essential. But it's telling that even when considering something quite serious, what we really want is to be entertained. So many of us don't want to think; we want to be amused and handed a quick fix.

Yet amusement only goes so far. When something happens to jar our thoughtlessness, we suddenly look up and look around. When life takes an alarming turn and we're flooded with emotions such as anger, fear, or despair, or when our behaviors have led to harm, we want answers. We want *real* help. We want meaning and purpose. Enter the church as the healing way station for those looking to make sense out of senselessness.

Shaken people walk into the church looking for wisdom and care. *Asking* for connection and answers. What a tremendous opportunity—and responsibility—for the caring person and for the community that offers those answers. What a tremendous moment to extend the outstretched hand of Jesus. As David Brooks describes,

> Wise people create a safe space where you can navigate the ambiguities and contradictions we all wrestle with. . . . Their essential gift is receptivity, the capacity to receive what you are sending. This is not a passive skill. The wise [listener] is not just keeping her ears open. She is creating an atmosphere of hospitality [that allows the help seeker] to set aside their fear of showing weakness, their fear of confronting themselves.[1]

As the person in pain opens their heart, the church can become the translator using the language of mental health. Through showing grace and love to someone who desperately needs it, we're invited to demonstrate that what the person really needs—the *only* thing that will truly heal their hurts—is Jesus.

Truth #2: You can't do it alone—and you don't have to.

A consistent theme offered by the more than two thousand pastors, church leaders, and mental health professionals in our research was the sheer scale of the need—and the reality that pastors and clinicians cannot address it alone. A pastor and leader in care ministry summarized the experience of so many clergy:

> Pastors have a lot of mouths to feed when it comes to ministries. Pastors are overwhelmed, and they're just trying to go and do what they're taught to do at seminary. Preach, do discipleship, youth ministry, worship, kids ministry. That's about what most pastors have the bandwidth to handle. And so even though it's important to have some sort of in-house mental health option, it sometimes feels like it's just one more thing that they have to do.

We find that this is a "Jethro moment." The church community can act toward pastors as Moses' father-in-law served him, asking, essentially, "Why do you have to do it alone?" (Exodus 18:14). Enlist others around you, and multiply yourself exponentially.

The same is true for clinicians, but with a different emphasis. Mental health professionals must acknowledge that the near-sacred "clinical hour" is insufficient to address the needs of society going forward. Ethically, clinicians have a mandate to creatively form strategies that address psychological needs. And when they're willing to do so, they can see the opportunity that exists in the church.

Truth #3: The church community can do this—and it works.

Given the long-standing default of professional referrals and the lack of history with lay mental health ministry, it's understandable that some pastors feel a bit unsure about how to do it. Which might lead to a bit of reluctance to start.

A psychologist who advocates for the creation of church ministry offered this reassurance:

> We can help churches by saying that the Bible is clear that we should be able to walk alongside people dealing with these issues. For example, it's like raising your kids. You don't have to have a degree in early childhood education! We can do this. It is all part of "one-anothering" in the church.

And as many leaders emphasized in our interviews, stepping into this space doesn't mean you have to have it all figured out at the beginning; you primarily have to find one or more people who are willing to help figure it out together. While hardly a church caregiver, General George Patton has resonance here: "Never tell people how to do things. Tell them what to do, and they will surprise you with their ingenuity."[2]

Multiple church leaders on our survey raised a very important point while considering this new area of ministry. One pastor said, "The one question I would most want to ask a leader already in this space is, What effect has mental health ministry had on the overall culture of your church?" Multiple church leaders questioned, "Would attention be taken away from discipleship and evangelism?"

So we asked those who already had these ministries. In chapter 3, we described one such leader, Nathan Graybill, the director of Watermark Church's re:generation program. In response to that question, he sent us reams of statistics. (As data nerds, we were very happy about this!) For example, in a study of more than 1,900 help seekers who completed this lay-led program, the participants reported:

trusting in God (96 percent)
experiencing freedom from their presenting struggle, such as anxiety or addiction (96 percent)
understanding how to deal with conflict well (93 percent)
forgiving others (94 percent)
receiving forgiveness from others (88 percent)
spending regular time in God's Word (85 percent)
experiencing trust in the church (80 percent)

Those are discipleship measures! And those outcomes arose from a purposeful program with trained and supervised lay helpers walking alongside those in need. There are *many* such purposeful programs today, including The Church Cares.

Imagine, one year from now, if those in *your* church were able to answer the same way as those respondents, and how it might change the culture.

The vision from the pastors and leaders to the church community is that it is *our* mission to be present in the challenges of people's lives. Not for the few who are "really ill" but for everyone. With an opportunity for astounding impact, not just among those coming to the church, but also among those who are already there.

Truth #4: The ultimate objective is to love as God loves . . . and to give ourselves away.

Reverend John Swinton has a PhD and is a pastor in the Church of Scotland, in addition to being a chair at the School of Divinity, History, Philosophy, and Art History at the University of Aberdeen. His advocacy for those in need through the care of the church has had an international impact. In an interview, one church leader shared a crucial concept from Swinton that she found so helpful—and that can help us overcome our reluctance to address mental health issues in the church.

She explained that when we say, "Oh, there's a person with mental illness," we get squirrelly. We assume that's not our wheelhouse. Maybe a professional should help them. Then she said, "But if you shift the emphasis and you say, 'Oh, there's a *person* with mental illness,' then suddenly it's like, 'That is the exact place the church needs to show up.' Because nobody knows how to take care of the person like the faith community. That's our job—to care for people."

The ideas articulated by Swinton are central to understanding the purpose of care ministry in the church. The subtitle of our book references the "mental health crisis." In these chapters, we've acknowledged that this is a serious social problem and offered ideas for how the church can play a major role in addressing and alleviating it. And not by hiring hundreds of thousands of counselors to attend to the many millions of people who can't receive the services they need.[3] Yes, the church can and should offer clinical help or referrals. But it has the capacity to do so much more—as part of the ultimate mission of the church.

In a podcast, Swinton said of the church,

> My general sense is that we need to think slightly differently about what health and healing look like. I always go back to that biblical understanding of health versus shalom. Because the Bible doesn't have an understanding of health as a biomedical absence of illness. The closest is the word *shalom* and what shalom has to do with righteousness, holiness, right relationship with God. And it includes friendship and community and prosperity and all sorts of different things. But the key thing is that health is being in right relationship with God. . . . It's not just me running around looking for ways I can fix you. And then blaming you when you're not fixed because you don't have enough faith or however you want to frame it. It actually has to do with me keeping you connected to Jesus. So what do I do in the midst of what you're going through, to ensure that you can be kept in touch with Jesus who has shalom in that way? And that takes you into a whole different way of thinking about relationships, community, and all these different things.[4]

Many pastors ask, "Of all the things going on in my church community, of all the other priorities, why should we offer this type of care ministry?" Our answer is this: because mental health ministry touches everything and will lead to an explosion of the exact discipleship and love you've been working to instill—and will take a weight off your shoulders. Because it's *through* the community of the church that humanity can experience shalom—the shalom that consists of right relationship with God.

People came to Jesus because of every physical and emotional issue imaginable—and as He brought healing, He gave them peace. Churches are called to do the same today.

APPENDIX 1

Legal Considerations for a Mental Health Ministry

If your church is planning to start a mental health ministry, here are three suggestions to consider, from a legal perspective. (Comprehensive resources pertaining to church and mental health legal concerns, written by David Velloney of Regent University School of Law, can be accessed at Thechurchcares.com.)

Articulate specific faith beliefs in church governing documents, including that care ministry is part of religious discipleship.

As religious institutions, churches in the US have the right to run their organization (and their counseling ministry) in accordance with their faith, without certain types of interference from the government. For example, the Constitution protects churches that desire to counsel people according to a traditionally biblical view of sexuality. But to help prevent a lawsuit or to protect a church that's being sued, those religious beliefs, positions, and processes ideally should be articulated in the church's governing documents, such as the church's charter, bylaws, and statement of faith.

Of course, every church will need to get the advice of a lawyer who knows local laws and regulations. But the text should probably include the point that care is viewed as religious discipleship among brothers and sisters in Christ, according to Matthew 28:19-20 ("Go and make disciples . . . teaching them to obey everything I have commanded you," NIV), rather than as arm's-length therapy between a clinician and a client.

In the helpful book *Legal Issues in Biblical Counseling*, one author makes this important point: "We must plainly distinguish our work as biblical counselors from the seemingly related work of the licensed therapist, and we must demonstrate that it is an essential part of our religious practice."[1] Although this book addresses the distinct practice of biblical counseling, the advice is similar for churches engaging in any sort of pastoral or lay counseling or coaching.

But what about churches that include licensed clinicians as part of their stable of resources? There may be several steps to follow, depending on what a lawyer advises based on state law. One step will likely be to make clear in both the church documents and the consent-for-care forms that these services provided by or within the church are viewed as religious discipleship just as much as or more than they are viewed as traditional therapy. As one specialized Christian lawyer told us, "When we are engaged in discipleship, we are constitutionally protected because we are primarily engaged in the practice of religion and helping one another conform to the image of Christ, rather than primarily engaged in the practice of trying to make someone happy."

Ensure that your intake process includes written informed consent.

As we discussed in chapter 6, all care must begin with written informed consent. This allows a caregiver (whether a professional or a layperson) to walk the person through the upcoming process and ensure that the help seeker understands and agrees with the plan.

The consent form captures in writing that the person acknowledges, for example, that this is lay counseling rather than professional therapy; that the church sees this as a discipleship process to help the person become more like Christ in their thoughts, feelings, and behaviors; and that the person agrees and is voluntarily participating in this process.

Ensure that the church insurance policy includes liability.

Insurance coverage can't prevent someone from suing a church, but it can help mitigate the effects of an unfounded lawsuit. Reach out to your insurance provider and be sure you understand what the policy covers and doesn't cover. And ensure that the provider understands the full perspective of the ministry of the church and what they are insuring. You can add or adjust coverage as necessary.

In all these areas, a pastor doesn't need to become a legal scholar in contracts or an expert on insurance. But the pastor and church leaders do need to ensure that they clarify whether this is "care ministry" or "running a counseling clinic" or both. That clarity of purpose and language will allow any church to define—for their people and for other parties—what *this* church is doing compared to the many other forms of ministry and therapy.

APPENDIX 2

Resources for Churches Building a Mental Health Ministry

with Charny Beck and Elisha Wisener

In this appendix, we have gathered a large number of resources and a list of ministries that are helpful for mental health and the church. We have placed it online so we can regularly update these resources.

This appendix is published online at Thechurchcares.com.

APPENDIX 3

How to Make a Referral

with Valter DeSouza

This appendix is designed to help a church determine whether a referral is needed and how to make one.

This appendix is published online at Thechurchcares.com.

Acknowledgments

This book, an organization, and an online clearinghouse of resources to empower the church have emerged because one pastor thought two strangers should talk. We met in early 2023 on a Zoom call organized by Dr. Jonathan Hoover—a friend and colleague of both of ours, who is a pastor as well as a professor at Regent University. Jonathan knew we both had a passion to see the power of the local church released to address the mental health crisis.

Since then, hundreds of people have assisted in building out this project—across all streams of the church, all philosophies of counseling and people-care, all ethnic groups and cultures, and all corners of the country (and beyond). How we wish we had the space to thank all of you by name! The names would scroll onward like the vast credits for a superhero movie, which is indeed how we think of all of you.

Your intelligence, creativity, passion, and vision were passed to us to be displayed on these pages. You helped us craft and review surveys, you sat for long interviews, you connected us to people we needed to speak with, you answered complicated questions, you provided guidance and insight, you shared nuanced details about your church's care model, you championed for your denomination or organization to be part of the survey, you did hours of coordination work to make it happen, you took the survey, you arranged interviews and focus groups, you reviewed and commented on drafts of this book, and on and on and on.

In this moment, we want to speak directly to each of you and express our deep, heartfelt gratitude for giving so much of your time, insight, skill, deep care for people, and love for the body of Christ.

There are a few people on our teams that we must individually thank.

On Shaunti's team, our deep thanks go to Shaunti's staff and operations director, Eileen Kirkland, as well as Charlyn Elliott for her number-crunching and survey skills, Amy Masaschi for the many hours of research arrangements, and Kristy Floyd, Laurie Davies, Samantha Griggs, and Nicole Owens for an immense amount of work on this project and beyond. Thanks to all of you for keeping everything running—and keeping Shaunti sane.

Jim's team at the Charis Institute at Regent University has built The Church Cares into a vibrant, active resource for every pastor. Most especially, our gratitude goes to Dr. Jennifer Ripley, the Charis co-director. In addition, Logan Battalini, Charny Beck, Sylvia Chipman, Valter DeSousa, Sarah Haught, Danny Holland, LaGaye McDowell, Stacie Otey-Scott, Steve Rawls, Reema Smith, and Dave Velloney were the idea generators and thought producers for this project. Your contributions emerge on every page.

Glen Moriarty and the 7 Cups team were able to help us think of a parallel universe using twenty-first century technology to reach the world with the gospel of hope. We are so grateful for Glen's vision and leadership, and to 7 Cups for building the technology to make the vision possible. Because of this, we are able to pass on to you, the reader, a starting point for how the church can harness technology to reach people.

To the generous major donor who is making this entire vision and initiative possible: we know you and your team want to remain anonymous . . . but you have our deep gratitude.

To the Tyndale family: we are so excited about working together on these important book projects. Our deep appreciation goes to Jan Long Harris, Jon Farrar, our amazingly talented and patient editor Stephanie Rische, our tenacious and skilled copyeditors Claire Lloyd and Stephanie Brockway, and everyone at the publisher who managed to create extra time in a publishing schedule that had none so we could launch the book well.

To Carey Nieuwhof: thank you for seeing the momentous opportunity before the church and championing this effort. We are so grateful.

Finally, our deep thanks go to our prayer teams, friends, and family members who have lifted us up in all the moments when it was desperately needed. Especially, we are grateful for our spouses, Jeff Feldhahn and Heather Sells. When we needed it most, you gave us encouragement, guidance, direction, prayer, and lots of coffee.

Ultimately, none of this would have happened were it not for the One who most cares about the lost and brokenhearted. May this work be used for the good of His people and for His glory.

Ad majorem Dei gloriam . . . all to the greater glory of God (1 Corinthians 10:31).

Notes

CHAPTER 1: A NEW WAY THROUGH

1. Unless otherwise specified, all names of people, places and organizations in this book are pseudonyms. Most quotes and illustrations used depict actual individuals and stories from the research process. Some individuals (such as Pastor Brent) are a compilation of several people and include combined, changed, or created details for purposes of illustration and/or protection of identity.
2. For simplicity, throughout this book we will refer to "church leaders" as meaning one or more of many different types of people who work in church contexts around mental health. This phrase of course denotes clergy, church staff, and church lay leaders. But it also includes a broad view of church-involved clinicians, coaches and other mental health professionals (licensed counselors, psychologists, biblical counselors, social workers, medical personnel, life coaches, etc.), as well as other roles such as denominational or diocesan officials, ministry leaders, and so on.
3. We titled the study "The Church Cares Project," and we will refer to it simply as "our survey" throughout the text.
4. Thomas Insel, "America's Mental Health Crisis," Trend, Pew, December 8, 2023, https://www.pewtrusts.org/en/trend/archive/fall-2023/americas-mental-health-crisis.
5. Christina Hoff Sommers and Sally Satel, *One Nation Under Therapy: How the Helping Culture Is Eroding Self-Reliance* (St. Martin's Press, 2005).
6. "Anxiety Disorders—Facts and Statistics," Anxiety and Depression Association of America, updated October 28, 2022, https://adaa.org/understanding-anxiety/facts-statistics.

7. In all presentations of data, "fully agreed" refers to the addition of "strongly agree" and "agree."
8. See "Health Workforce Projections" as of November 2024, from the Health Resources & Services Administration, https://bhw.hrsa.gov/data-research/projecting-health-workforce-supply-demand.
9. The National Institute of Mental Health estimates that serious mental illness makes up about 6 percent of the adult population. See "Mental Illness," National Institute of Mental Health, updated September 2024, https://www.nimh.nih.gov/health/statistics/mental-illness.
10. Carey Nieuwhof, https://careynieuwhof.com.
11. James N. Sells, Amy Trout, and Heather C. Sells, *Beyond the Clinical Hour: How Counselors Can Partner with the Church to Address the Mental Health Crisis* (InterVarsity Press, 2024).
12. *Our Epidemic of Loneliness and Isolation: The U.S. Surgeon General's Advisory on the Healing Effects of Social Connection and Community* (U.S. Department of Health and Human Services, 2023), https://www.hhs.gov/sites/default/files/surgeon-general-social-connection-advisory.pdf. The report also states, "Across many measures, Americans appear to be becoming less socially connected. . . . This is not a new problem—certain declines have been occurring for decades." Further, Statista, an online data service, reports that the number of single-person households in the US was just 6.9 percent in 1960. In 2023 it was about 38.1 percent. "Number of Single-Person Households in the United States from 1960 to 2023," Statista, November 2023, https://www.statista.com/statistics/242022/number-of-single-person-households-in-the-us/.
13. Isabel Goddard, "What Does Friendship Look like in America?" Pew Research Center, October 12, 2023, https://www.pewresearch.org/short-reads/2023/10/12/what-does-friendship-look-like-in-america/.
14. Daniel A. Cox, "Men's Social Circles Are Shrinking," Survey Center on American Life, June 29, 2021, https://www.americansurveycenter.org/why-mens-social-circles-are-shrinking/.
15. Berna Güroğlu, "The Power of Friendship: The Developmental Significance of Friendships from a Neuroscience Perspective," *Child Development Perspectives* 16, no. 2 (2022): 111, https://srcd.onlinelibrary.wiley.com/doi/10.1111/cdep.12450.
16. For example, see Joseph D. Hovey et al., "Religion-Based Emotional Social Support Mediates the Relationship Between Intrinsic Religiosity and Mental Health," *Archives of Suicide Research* 18, no. 4 (2014): 376–391, https://www.tandfonline.com/doi/abs/10.1080/13811118.2013.833149.

17. William Heseltine-Carp and Mathew Hoskins, "Clergy as a Frontline Mental Health Service: A UK Survey of Medical Practitioners and Clergy," *General Psychiatry* 33, no. 6 (October 23, 2020): e100229, https://pmc.ncbi.nlm.nih.gov/articles/PMC7590374/.
18. Stephen Grcevich, "Mental Health Ministry as an Evangelism and Outreach Strategy," *Outreach*, October 11, 2023, https://outreachmagazine.com/features/77760-mental-health-ministry-as-an-evangelism-and-outreach-strategy.html.
19. Ed Stetzer, "Why Churches Without Broken People Are Broken," *Outreach*, September 21, 2023, https://outreachmagazine.com/features/68614-why-churches-without-broken-people-are-broken.html.
20. Mark Griffiths, *One Generation from Extinction: How the Church Connects with the Unchurched Child* (Monarch Books, 2019).
21. J. Henry Harris, *Robert Raikes: The Man Who Founded the Sunday School* (The National Sunday School Union, 1930).
22. Harris, *Robert Raikes.*

CHAPTER 2: FIVE CHURCHES THAT ARE DOING IT WELL

1. Unless otherwise stated, most identifying details in examples, stories, and quotes have been removed or changed, and in some cases they've been combined. Quotes have been edited for length and clarity.
2. As noted, unless otherwise specified, all names of people and organizations in this book are pseudonyms. The amazing leaders and churches that form the basis for these case studies have our deep gratitude. We are purposefully not naming them, as we saw these types of examples across all streams of the church and don't want to give the impression that any particular church culture is the provenance of any particular approach. We were grateful to see these ideas spring up across the body of Christ in all its diversity and beauty.
3. "Health Workforce Shortage Areas," Health Resources and Services Administration, dashboard as of January 22, 2025, https://data.hrsa.gov/topics/health-workforce/shortage-areas.

CHAPTER 3: THE STATE OF THE CHURCH

1. According to 2023 Gallup data, 32 percent of the population had attended a worship service in the last seven days, with 30 percent saying they attended every week or almost every week. "Religion," Gallup, accessed December 27, 2024, https://news.gallup.com/poll/1690/Religion.aspx.

2. Note that the data analysis in this book was conducted on the primary English-language survey, with spot checks on the Spanish-language version to compare the samples. (For example, two-thirds of the data were from pastors in both samples.) Statistically, combining the two samples would not change the conclusions.
3. This number includes those who responded with "strongly agree," "agree," or "somewhat agree/somewhat disagree."
4. "Health Workforce Shortage Areas," Health Resources and Services Administration, dashboard as of September 22, 2024, https://data.hrsa.gov/topics/health-workforce/shortage-areas. Per the HRSA dashboard, as of 9/22/24, 123 million people lived in a Health Professional Shortage Area (HPSA). As of 9/22/24, the Census Bureau "U.S. and World Population Clock" estimated the U.S. population at 337 million. Thus, 36% lived in HPSA areas.
5. Ching-Fang Sun et al., "Low Availability, Long Wait Times, and High Geographic Disparity of Psychiatric Outpatient Care in the US," *General Hospital Psychiatry* 84 (September 2023): 12–17, https://pubmed.ncbi.nlm.nih.gov/37290263/.
6. "Health Workforce Projections," Health Resources and Services Administration, as of March 2024, https://bhw.hrsa.gov/data-research/projecting-health-workforce-supply-demand. (This page's resources are continually updated.)

CHAPTER 4: BUILDING A CARING CHURCH MINISTRY

1. We use the terms "helpers" and "caregivers" as synonymous throughout the book.
2. See Mental Health America's "Access to Care Data, 2022," accessed January 28, 2025, https://mhanational.org/issues/2022/mental-health-america-access-care-data.
3. We suggest the Association of Biblical Counselors, https://christiancounseling.com/; the Biblical Counseling and Spiritual Formation Network (a division of the American Association of Christian Counselors), https://aacc.net/product/biblical-counseling-spiritual-formation/; and the Biblical Counseling Coalition, https://www.biblicalcounselingcoalition.org/.
4. *The Avengers*, directed by Joss Whedon (Marvel Studios, 2012); "*The Avengers*: Quotes," IMDb, accessed January 7, 2025, https://www.imdb.com/title/tt0848228/quotes/.

CHAPTER 5: "BUT WHAT ABOUT . . . ?"

1. Warren Buffett to Berkshire Hathaway shareholders, February 25, 1985, Berkshire Hathaway Inc., https://www.berkshirehathaway.com/letters/1984.html.
2. Carol Pipes, "Henry Blackaby, the Christian Writer Who Impacted Millions of Lives Through *Experiencing God* Bible Study, Has Died," *Christian Index*, February 11, 2024, https://christianindex.org/stories/henry-blackaby-the-christian-writer-who-impacted-millions-of-lives-through-experiencing-god,73365.
3. As examples, see Siang-Yang Tan et al., "Lay Counseling: A Brief Review and Update from a Christian Perspective," *Journal of Psychology and Christianity* 42, no. 3 (2023): 251–258, https://research.ebsco.com/linkprocessor/plink?id=ff014d06-d2db-3d7d-b23d-3a7fce5e69f6; Daisy R. Singla et al., "Democratizing Access to Psychological Therapies: Innovations and the Role of Psychologists," *Journal of Consulting and Clinical Psychology* 91, no. 11 (2023): 623–625, https://psycnet.apa.org/fulltext/2024-14058-001.html; K. D. Smith et al., "The Use of Paraprofessional Service Delivery in Psychological Helping Settings: Comparative Effectiveness and Considerations," *Professional Psychology: Research and Practice* 55, no. 6 (2024): 573–583, https://psycnet.apa.org/doi/10.1037/pro0000597; Siang-Yang Tan et al., *Lay Counseling: Equipping Christians for a Helping Ministry*, rev. ed. (Zondervan, 2016).
4. P. G. Northouse, *Leadership: Theory and Practice*, rev. ed. (Sage, 2021), 213–215.
5. "Dixon Chibanda: Grandmothers Help to Scale Up Mental Health Care," *Bulletin of the World Health Organization* 96, no. 6 (June 1, 2018): 376–377, https://pmc.ncbi.nlm.nih.gov/articles/PMC5996204/.
6. "Dixon Chibanda: Grandmothers Help to Scale Up Mental Health Care."
7. Robert R. Carkhuff and Charles B. Truax, "Lay Mental Health Counseling. The Effects of Lay Group Counseling," *Journal of Consulting Psychology* 29, no. 5 (1965): 426–431, https://pubmed.ncbi.nlm.nih.gov/5827511/.
8. These numbers do not include those who said these options did not apply/other or weren't sure.

CHAPTER 6: BEST PRACTICES IN MENTAL HEALTH MINISTRY

1. "The Real Story Behind Apple's 'Think Different' Campaign," *Forbes*, December 14, 2011, https://www.forbes.com/sites/onmarketing/2011/12/14/the-real-story-behind-apples-think-different-campaign/.

2. For example, in 2024, of those who use digital technology, about 96.2 percent accessed the internet via mobile devices. See "Share of Users Worldwide Accessing the Internet in Second Quarter 2024, by Device," Statista, November 5, 2024, https://www.statista.com/statistics/1289755/internet-access-by-device-worldwide/.
3. Ritesh Mistry et al., "Parenting-Related Stressors and Self-Reported Mental Health of Mothers with Young Children," *American Journal of Public Health* 97 no. 7 (July 1, 2007): 1261–1268, https://ajph.aphapublications.org/doi/full/10.2105/AJPH.2006.088161.
4. Rebecca J. McCloskey and Fei Pei, "The Role of Parenting Stress in Mediating the Relationship Between Neighborhood Social Cohesion and Depression and Anxiety Among Mothers of Young Children in Fragile Families," *Journal of Community Psychology* 47, no. 4 (2019): 869–881, https://pmc.ncbi.nlm.nih.gov/articles/PMC6472962/.
5. *The Princess Bride*, directed by Rob Reiner (Act III Communications, 1987).
6. The *2014 ACA Code of Ethics* from the American Counseling Association says, "B.1.c. Respect for Confidentiality. Counselors protect the confidential information of prospective and current clients. Counselors disclose information only with appropriate consent or with sound legal or ethical justification," American Counseling Association, https://www.counseling.org/docs/default-source/ethics/2014-aca-code-of-ethics.pdf.
7. The *2014 ACA Code of Ethics* from the American Counseling Association reads: "B.3.b. Interdisciplinary Teams. When services provided to the client involve participation by an interdisciplinary or treatment team, the client will be informed of the team's existence and composition, information being shared, and the purposes of sharing such information."
8. Kristen Kansiewicz, "Connecting Pastors and Counselors," Church Therapy Associates, October 22, 2017, https://www.churchtherapy.com/2017/10/22/connecting-pastors-and-counselors/.
9. The American Counseling Association's *2014 Code of Ethics* section B.3.b says that in a situation where a caregiver is part of a team and something is exposed in counseling that they don't know how to handle, they can share it with their superiors. Confidentiality includes consultation with an identified treatment team.
10. See PastorServe, accessed January 9, 2025, https://pastorserve.org.
11. Lifeway Research, *Pastors' Views on Mental Illness* (Lifeway Research, 2022), https://research.lifeway.com/wp-content/uploads/2022/08/Pastors-Sept-2021-Mental-Illness-Report.pdf.

12. Kristen Kansiewicz, "Attitudes Toward Seeking Professional Counseling Among Assemblies of God Ministers in the United States," (PhD diss., Regent University, 2021). This study of AOG pastors confirms other research within Baptist and Methodist denominations, as cited in her writings.

PART 2 INTRODUCTION

1. James R. Rogers and Karen M. Soyka, "Grace and Compassion at Ground Zero," *Crisis: The Journal of Crisis Intervention and Suicide Prevention* 25, no. 1 (2004), 27, https://psycnet.apa.org/record/2004-13098-005.

CHAPTER 7: THE NECESSARY PEOPLE

1. Gary Burnison, "Coaches Don't Win Games," *Briefings*, no. 33 (2017): 6–7, https://www.kornferry.com/insights/briefings-magazine/issue-33/on-leadership.
2. We're aware that *not* stepping into one corner or the other may itself be viewed by some as taking a contrary position. This is where we ask for grace, just as we suggest that grace be offered to others who are trying to care and heal in the name of Jesus.
3. Gaura Lohani and Pragya Sharma, "Effect of Clinical Supervision on Self-Awareness and Self-Efficacy of Psychotherapists and Counselors: A Systematic Review," *Psychological Services* 20, no. 2 (2023): 291, https://psycnet.apa.org/record/2022-86139-001.
4. *MADtv*, season 6, episode 24, aired May 12, 2001, on Fox; see "Bob Newhart—STOP IT! The best two word coaching you'll ever get," posted April 20, 2024, YouTube, 6 min., 4 sec., https://www.youtube.com/watch?v=bcSAQyzPcl0.
5. Paul David Tripp, *Instruments in the Redeemer's Hands: People in Need of Change Helping People in Need of Change* (P&R Publishing, 2002), 117.

CHAPTER 8: LISTENING

1. For more information on the evidence of activity, see Jane Williams et al., "Can Physical Activity Support Grief Outcomes in Individuals Who Have Been Bereaved? A Systematic Review," *Sports Medicine – Open* 7, no. 1 (April 8, 2021): 26, https://pubmed.ncbi.nlm.nih.gov/33830368/.
2. Williams et al., "Can Physical Activity Support Grief Outcomes in Individuals Who Have Been Bereaved?"

CHAPTER 9: MANAGING EMOTIONS

1. Gary Thomas, *Sacred Marriage: What if God Designed Marriage to Make Us Holy More Than to Make Us Happy?* (Zondervan, 2000).
2. Gary Thomas, text message to authors, November 1, 2024.
3. Tristram Jones, James N. Sells, and Mark Rehfuss, "How Wounded the Healers? The Prevalence of Relapse Among Addiction Counselors in Recovery from Alcohol and Other Drugs," *Alcoholism Treatment Quarterly* 27, no. 4 (2009): 389–408, https://www.tandfonline.com/doi/full/10.1080/07347320903209863. Note that although the study found that wounded healers can make great caregivers, they also have a high relapse rate (38%). These caregivers may require additional support themselves.
4. Jones et al., "How Wounded the Healers?"
5. Shaunti Feldhahn, *The Surprising Secrets of Highly Happy Marriages: The Little Things That Make a Big Difference* (Multnomah Books, 2013), 109.
6. Many versions of this prayer exist, as do many claims to its authoring and adaptation—possibly as far back as hieroglyphics on Egyptian obelisks. Dr. Niebuhr's 1932 version appears to be the most clearly identified. See https://www.aa.org/sites/default/files/literature/assets/smf-129_en.pdf.

CHAPTER 10: HEALING RELATIONSHIPS

1. Megan Fate Marshman, *Relaxed: Walking with the One Who Is Not Worried About a Thing* (Zondervan Books, 2024).
2. You can find a detailed description of "the four horsemen" at the Gottman Institute website as well as in their publications on couples care. See Ellie Lisitsa, "The Four Horsemen: Criticism, Contempt, Defensiveness, and Stonewalling," Gottman Institute, updated October 15, 2024, https://www.gottman.com/blog/the-four-horsemen-recognizing-criticism-contempt-defensiveness-and-stonewalling/.
3. Bob Smietana, "Pastors More Likely to Address Domestic Violence, Still Lack Training," Lifeway Research, September 18, 2018, https://research.lifeway.com/2018/09/18/pastors-more-likely-to-address-domestic-violence-still-lack-training/.
4. Sarah J. White et al., "Global Prevalence and Mental Health Outcomes of Intimate Partner Violence Among Women: A Systematic Review and Meta-Analysis," Trauma, Violence, and Abuse 25, no. 1 (February 24, 2023): 494–511, https://pmc.ncbi.nlm.nih.gov/articles/PMC10666489/.
5. For example, Emerson Eggerichs, *Love and Respect in the Family: The Respect Parents Desire; The Love Children Need* (W Publishing, 2013).

6. See the 30-Day Kindness Challenge portal at https://www.jointhekindnesschallenge.com/; see also Shaunti Feldhahn, *The Kindness Challenge: Thirty Days to Improve Any Relationship* (Waterbrook, 2016).

CHAPTER 11: ADDRESSING ADDICTIONS

1. *Amazing Grace*, directed by Michael Apted (Samuel Goldwyn Films, 2006), https://tv.apple.com/us/movie/amazing-grace/umc.cmc.7563e2027sxa989hkvpqcv5lj?playableId=tvs.sbd.9001%3A270356352.

CHAPTER 12: ADDRESSING TRAUMA AND GRIEF

1. Richard Langer et al., "Theological Perspectives on Trauma: Human Flourishing After the Fall," in *Treating Trauma in Christian Counseling*, ed. Heather Davediuk Gingrich and Fred C. Gingrich (IVP Academic, 2017).
2. Kenneth I. Pargament and Julie J. Exline, *Working with Spiritual Struggles in Psychotherapy: From Research to Practice* (Guilford Press, 2022).
3. Langer et al., "Theological Perspectives on Trauma," 52.
4. "How Common Is PTSD in Adults?," PTSD: National Center for PTSD, U.S. Department of Veterans Affairs, accessed January 14, 2025, https://www.ptsd.va.gov/understand/common/common_adults.asp.
5. GriefShare resources can be located at https://www.griefshare.org/.
6. Information regarding group resources provided by American Bible Society's Trauma Healing Institute can be found at https://traumahealinginstitute.org/lead-a-group.

CONCLUSION: EQUIPPING THE CHURCH TO TRANSFORM THE WORLD

1. David Brooks, *How to Know a Person: The Art of Seeing Others Deeply and Being Deeply Seen* (Random House, 2023), 324.
2. We Are The Mighty, "11 Gen. George Patton Quotes That Show His Strategic Awesomeness," Military.com, August 5, 2021, https://www.military.com/history/2021/08/05/11-general-george-patton-quotes-show-his-strategic-awesomeness.html.
3. See James N. Sells et al., "The Hurrier I Go, the Behinder I Get: Unpacking the Surge in Mental Health Concerns," chap. 2 in *Beyond the Clinical Hour: How Counselors Can Partner with the Church to Address the Mental Health Crisis* (InterVarsity Press, 2024).
4. John Swinton, *Sanctuary Mental Health,* podcast, season 1, episode 1, "Breaking the Mold," January 30, 2020, https://sanctuarymentalhealth.org/2020/01/30/john-swinton/. Edited for clarity.

APPENDIX 1: LEGAL CONSIDERATIONS FOR A MENTAL HEALTH MINISTRY

1. Edward Charles Wilde, "Truth in Advertising: Communicating About Your Counseling Ministry with Clarity," in *Legal Issues in Biblical Counseling: Direction and Help for Churches and Counselors*, ed. T. Dale Johnson Jr. and Edward Charles Wilde (New Growth Press, 2022), 47.

About the Authors

Shaunti Feldhahn is a bestselling author, popular speaker, and social researcher known for her groundbreaking work to help people flourish in life, faith, leadership, and relationships. Her research-based books, such as *The Good News About Marriage*, *For Women Only*, *For Men Only*, and *Find Rest*, are filled with surprising and practical insights, selling more than three million copies in twenty-five languages.

Shaunti holds a graduate degree from Harvard University, where she met her husband, Jeff (who graduated from Harvard Law School), by literally bumping into him in Harvard Square. She started out on Wall Street before unexpectedly diving into social research. Shaunti speaks at dozens of events each year to women, couples (usually with Jeff), and Christian leaders, sharing her fascinating research findings about the transformative little truths that make a big difference. (See Shaunti.com for more.)

Shaunti and Jeff have two amazing kids in their early twenties who are figuring out adulting. The family lives in Atlanta, Georgia, and enjoys every minute of life at warp speed.

James (Jim) N. Sells, PhD, is a Hughes Endowed Chair of Mental Health and Christian Thought, a licensed psychologist, and a professor of counseling at Regent University, Virginia Beach, Virginia. He codirects the Charis Institute, which is a research, training, and resource center for all things related to the church, marriage, family, and mental health.

He received his BA from Biola University and has MAs from Wheaton College and NIU. His PhD is in counseling psychology from the University of Southern California. Dr. Sells consults and advises pastors and ministry leaders in increasing effectiveness, and he teaches graduates how to become effective therapists and visionary leaders in Christian mental health.

He is the author/coauthor of many books, including *Family Therapies*, *Counseling Couples in Conflict*, *Beyond the Clinical Hour*, and *Ministering to Families in Crisis*. His research focuses on creating effective care ministries, marital restoration and family therapy, and forgiveness and reconciliation.

Jim is married to Heather, and they live in the Tidewater area of Virginia and North Carolina. Their three children are adults and are responding to God's call on their lives, forming their purpose, and creating their families. Jim loves trying to fix things that don't work well, whether that's relationships, houses, cars, or squeaky doors.